MW00577779

Presbyterianism in West Virginia

A History

DENNIS ELDON BILLS

Presbyterianism in West Virginia: A History

Copyright © 2019 by Dennis Eldon Bills. All rights reserved.

Published by

ReformingWV Publications
716 Park Ave.
New Martinsville WV 26155

ReformingWV Publications provides print and digital resources in the Reformed tradition with the goal of increasing the influence of Reformed Theology in the great state of West Virginia. Online at reformingwv.org.

Cover photo by Dennis E. Bills: Old Stone Church Door and Plaque.

Unless otherwise noted, all photos are by Dennis E. Bills.

ISBN-10: 1-7337280-1-5

ISBN-13: 978-1-7337280-1-0

To the Churches of the New River Presbytery
of the Presbyterian Church in America:

Grace Church, Buckhannon
Christ Community Church, Fairmont
Covenant Presbyterian Church, Nitro
Kanawha Salines Presbyterian Church, Malden
Mercy Presbyterian Church, Morgantown
Pliny Presbyterian Church, Pliny
Providence Reformed Presbyterian Church, Barboursville
Redeemer Presbyterian Church, Hurricane
Trinity Presbyterian Church, New Martinsville
Winifrede Presbyterian Church, Winifrede

May I here hazard a conjecture that has often occurred to me since I inhabited this place, that nature has designed this part of the world a peaceable retreat for some of her favorite children, where pure morals will be preserved by separating them from other societies at so respectful a distance by ridges of mountains; and I sincerely wish time may prove my conjecture rational and true.

Colonel John Stuart
Lewisburg, Virginia
July 15, 1798

Although Presbyterianism has progressed but slowly in the region in which we set up our banner; still, if we look at the situation of the country, the difficulties that were to be encountered, and the means employed to accomplish the end, the wonder will be that it succeeded at all.

The Rev. Dr. John McElhenney
Lewisburg, Virginia
April 12, 1838

It is the duty of the church collectively, and of particular portions of it, and of individuals, so to preserve the records of his dealings with them, that they may be able to remember all the way in which the Lord God has led them. There is a large amount of history floating in the traditions of congregations and families, which is constantly perishing from off the earth, as one and another of the more aged are gathered to their fathers. We are, today, attempting to gather up some of these traditions and recollections that more especially concern us, that we may remember the way in which the Lord God has led us.

Rev. McElhenney
Lewisburg, Virginia
June 5, 1858

CONTENTS

PREFACE

This project has been a work of passion—by a minister for ministers, a Presbyterian for Presbyterians, and a West Virginian for West Virginians. For that reason, I humbly beg the forbearance of those who immediately recognize it is not the work of a trained historian or academic scholar. It seems the work of writing Presbyterian histories has mostly fallen upon ministers. By that qualification at least, I presume to join their ranks. I wish I were more of a scholar, but I humbly hope this book, such as it is, does both Presbyterianism and my beloved West Virginia proud.

The book began as an adaptation of my doctoral project at Pittsburgh Theological Seminary, titled "An Unobstructed Educational Model for Ministerial Candidates of the New River Presbytery of the Presbyterian Church in America." For obvious reasons, I intended the adaptation only for my presbytery. As I wrote and edited, though, I quickly realized that the project could be improved by the addition of a chapter on the history of Presbyterianism in West Virginia. As the new chapter grew, the entire project changed—the substitute motion became the main motion, as it were (Let the Presbyterian reader understand!). In the end, I felt a history might be of greater benefit and wider interest than the adaptation, though I did manage to salvage a few thesis paragraphs here and there.

I am grateful for the help of many people and organizations. First are the Appalachian Presbyterian ministers or historians whose works are liberally footnoted throughout. My heavy reliance upon regional authors is quite intentional, even for some of the broader strokes of Presbyterian history. They worked with primary sources in ways I had neither the ability nor opportunity to do. I am in awe of (and humbled by) their skills, and their work deserves to be kept in the light.

I also wish to thank Wayne Sparkman, Director of the PCA Historical Center, for his feedback and for lending me the *Inventory of the Church Archives of West Virginia: The Presbyterian Church*; Lee Ann Blair of West Virginia Northern Community College who patiently processed my inter-library loan requests; Jim-Bob Williams of Providence Reformed Presbyterian Church in Barboursville who chauffeured me to sites in Charleston; the Greenbrier Historical Society for tracking down answers from the archives; West Virginia State Delegate Larry Rowe who supported, advised, and encouraged my research. I commend to the reader his forthcoming books on Booker T. Washington and the history of Malden. Thanks as well to the many churches that helped or hosted me during my research. My deepest gratitude goes to my wife Kathi. Thank you for being so patient with me. Only you, our boys, and God know how consuming this project has been. I am so very grateful for everyone's help, though any errors are my own.

Histories select and interpret according to the writer's purposes and passions. I studied to answer my own questions, with hope that others might share those same questions. My book therefore provides a confessional perspective on Presbyterian history prior to the rise of modernism, which is to say that it generally ends around the turn of the twentieth century, though there are some exceptions. As far as I know, the chapter on presbytery history in West Virginia (Chapter 4) has never before been set down in one place. Neither has the intersection of Presbyterianism and the African-American experience in West Virginia (Chapter 7). Nevertheless, a future edition could be greatly improved by adding chapters on twentieth century developments; the key roles of Presbyterian women as wives, mothers, missionaries, educators, and trailblazers of benevolence and temperance societies; and pioneer theology, praxis, and preaching.

The year 2019 is providential for this publication because it is the bicentennial of three of our most significant churches (highlighted within as the "Three Kanawha Valley Churches"). I would like this to be my contribution to their celebrations. However, I especially dedicate this book to my presbytery, a rather small but wonderful group of gospel-believing churches, elders, and church members. I humbly submit it to them for their encouragement, education, and edification. To any other readers, Presbyterian or not, I bid you "Godspeed in the common cause." Perhaps you might take time to visit one of the churches listed on the dedication page. Hopefully there will be many more in years to come.

Finally, I hope this history will come to the attention of our evangelical Presbyterian judicatories, colleges, and seminaries. There was a time when the Presbyterian Church said to us, "You shall occupy a portion of this State which lies west of the Alleghany Mountains." My prayer is that our great West Virginia history might inspire and convict the nation's Presbyterians to once again turn their eyes upon Central Appalachia to train candidates for ministry on the western waters.

D.E.B
New Martinsville, West Virginia
March 14, 2019

1

THE SETTLEMENT OF THE WESTERN WATERS

PRESBYTERIANISM FOLLOWED THE PATHS of the settlers into West Virginia. The "Scotch-Irish" brought their religion with them and founded some of the first churches west of the Alleghenies. Their preachers carried the Gospel on horseback to homesteads along countless creek bottoms and river valleys. They "set the people in church order" in every place and pastored them through schisms that cleaved nations and denominations. They erected presbyteries and synods for the stated purpose of "meeting more effectively an opportunity in home missions which we believe is without parallel within the bounds of our church."[1] When Greenbrier Presbytery was organized in 1838, the Reverend Dr. John McElhenney—one of several fathers and brothers this small book will restore to our memory—preached that "every member of this presbytery must measurably assume the character of a missionary."[2] More than two centuries since our first churches were organized, the hollows are an unreached mission field once again. May this brief history exemplify

---

[1] Lloyd McFarland Courtney, *The Church on the Western Waters: An History of Greenbrier Presbytery and Its Churches* (Richmond: Whittet & Shepperson, 1940), 57. Hereafter, *Greenbrier.*
[2] Rose W. Fry, *Recollections of the Rev. John McElhenney, D.D.* (Richmond VA: Whittet and Shepherdson, 1893), 233. Hereafter, *Recollections.*

and inspire the work that will resettle Presbyterianism in the hills of West Virginia.

In the early 1700s, West Virginia was the western frontier of the British Colonies. It was a wild and wonderful wilderness blocked off from the rest of Virginia by the Alleghenies. The rivers to the west of the mountains flowed away from the coast—into the Ohio River Basin—signaling to early explorers that the land on the other side was a different world. For a while it was known as "the land on the western waters."[3]

The floodgates into this new land, however, did not fully open until the last quarter of the eighteenth century. Through the 1740s, the western waters' main inhabitants were Indians, and its only British-colonial visitors were trappers, traders, and adventurers. By mid-century, pioneers had begun to filter through the Allegheny mountains in fits and starts, but they faced several obstacles that kept the rate of migration slow until the end of the century.

The first obstacle was the Allegheny mountain range itself. Rugged, corrugated mountains were an almost impenetrable barrier that stretched for hundreds of miles and formed a massive rear wall against which the growing Colony of Virginia was uncomfortably pressed.[4]

---

[3] The colonial and early American term *western waters* (generally uncapitalized) occurs in the literature as common parlance but without definition. Its usage appears synonymous with *western rivers,* or the Ohio and Mississippi rivers and their combined watersheds. When referring specifically to the Trans-Allegheny frontier, it appears to mean *any and all* land within the colonial Virginia territory between the Ohio River and the Allegheny mountains (which today includes West Virginia). Thus, early residents of what are now Greenbrier and Barbour Counties, for example, referred to their own regions as *the western waters,* even though each was at least 150 miles from the Ohio River. The use of the term to designate such a vast, landlocked area underscores how essential river valleys were for gaining entry into the rugged West Virginia interior.

[4] The Appalachian Mountains contain three land features that bear upon the history of pioneer expansion into West Virginia: The Blue Ridge Mountains, the Great Appalachian Valley, and the Allegheny Mountains. The Blue Ridge Mountains form the eastern edge of the Appalachian Mountain range in Virginia. The Allegheny

Only a few years before had settlers finally crossed the Blue Ridge mountains that ran parallel to the Alleghenies, into the vast Valley of Virginia that lay between. From 1740 until 1755, the only infiltrators through the westernmost mountains were small groups of pioneers who trekked across barely passable gaps and trails. In 1755, an ancient Indian trail through the Cumberland Narrows was expanded by the colonial military on its way to an unfortunate battle with the French near what is now Pittsburgh. The improved road allowed land speculators and settlers to begin crossing more frequently into the many river valleys of the western waters.

The second obstacle to migration was the French and Indian War of 1756. Nearly a century before, the French had claimed the Trans-Allegheny region for themselves. Faced with repeated British-colonial encroachments, they enjoined the Native Americans to aid their defense. Indian raids extended deep into West Virginia territory, killing many pioneer families and forcing most others to flee. What few stayed behind were under constant threat of massacre. Many did not survive. The battle between the French and the British quickly escalated into the world-wide Seven Years' War. On the war's other fronts, France was no match for the British and eventually ceded the western waters in the Treaty of Paris in 1763.

The Indians did not surrender though; they had been fighting for more than the French. So Britain immediately issued a royal proclamation forbidding settlement west of the Alleghenies to curtail an expensive conflict with the Native Americans. But the

---

Mountains, running parallel to the Blue Ridge, formed the western inhabited border of the Colony of Virginia in the mid-1700s. In between lay the Great Appalachian Valley, which was known as the Valley of Virginia, the Shenandoah Valley, or simply, "the Valley." It was this valley that "filled up" with Scots-Irish migrants who of necessity overflowed westward through Jefferson, Berkeley and Hampshire Counties.

Proclamation Line was difficult to enforce. Colonists once again began dripping into the region, inciting the Indians to protect their hunting lands.

Thus the hostile Indian population continued to provide yet a third obstacle to migration. Off and on for thirty years, warriors and pioneers skirmished in the vast wilderness between the Ohio River and the Alleghenies. Hundreds died on both sides, increasing bitterness and racial tensions. Appalachian history records ugly stories of beautiful, serene valleys where Indians killed entire families, including women and children. Just as horribly, it also testifies to the evil actions of presumptuous settlers who retaliated against Indians without measure or discrimination.[5] It was a brutal and fearful era for both sides.

After the Revolutionary War commenced, the Indians once again took sides against the colonists. But as they had following the French and Indian War, they continued fighting after the British surrendered in 1783.[6] Finally, their largest coalition was defeated by Mad Anthony Wayne in 1793 at the Battle of Fallen Timbers in western Ohio. The ensuing treaty removed the Indian threat far from West Virginia, and the floodgates to the Trans-Allegheny frontier finally opened. Settlers poured over the mountains in droves. At the time, West Virginia contained only 56,000 people. Twenty years later, the population had nearly doubled. By the Civil War, it had increased to almost 377,000.[7]

---

[5] For example, the murder of Chief Cornstalk, the Yellow Creek massacre, the Gnadenhutten massacre, and Cresap's War.

[6] For the riveting account of how the Shawnee Indians attacked, kidnapped, or murdered members of a Presbyterian family during this time, see James Moore Brown, *The Captives of Abb's Valley: Revised and Annotated,* ed. Dennis Eldon Bills (New Martinsville WV: ReformingWV Publications, 2019). Republished as one of the few books written by a Presbyterian minister from West Virginia to give insight into pioneer culture and context.

[7] Richard L. Forstall, *Population of States and Counties of the United States: 1790-1990* (Washington, DC: U.S. Bureau of the Census, 1996).

Table 1 1790 Population and Migration Routes

	County	Population	River Valley
East of the Alleghenies	Berkeley	19,713	Potomac
	Hampshire	7,346	Cacapon
	Hardy	7,336	Cacapon
	Pendleton	2,452	South Branch Potomac
Total East		36,847	
West of the Alleghenies	Randolph	951	Tygart/Cheat
	Greenbrier	6,015	Greenbrier
	Monongalia	4,768	Monongahela/Tygart
	Harrison	2,080	Monongahela/Tygart
	Ohio	5,212	Ohio
Total West		19,026	
State Total		55,873	

Initially, rugged terrain forced settlers to follow only the winding routes of the western water's many river valleys. In these valleys and hollers, alongside creeks and rivers, the pioneers established the first growing settlements.[8] By 1790, the population of West Virginia was concentrated throughout only nine counties (Table 1), all of which were in or near river valleys. The rest of the territory would have to wait until the Virginia Assembly could levy taxes and open new roads through mountains. In these valleys and hollers, and in these settlements, the Presbyterians began gathering to worship, first under the shelter of groves of trees and then in rough-hewn log meeting-houses. Not long after, these *Societies of Christians Called Presbyterians* began crying out for preachers to minister the Word and Sacrament.

---

[8] For the uninitiated, a "holler," "holla," or hollow is a small valley that runs perpendicular to a larger valley. This recessed break in a line of mountains or hills forms a watershed with a creek or "run" at "the bottom." The "head" is the deepest point of the hollow. The "mouth" is where the creek or hollow opens into the larger valley. To go "up the holler" is to go toward the head; "down the holler" is toward the mouth.

2

THE PRESBYTERIAN PIONEERS

THOSE WHO INITIALLY POURED across the Allegheny Mountains were a hardy sort, with uncommon traits and common heritages. Most of them were immigrants trying to make a place for themselves in a new land. They had left a life of hard living and were prepared to live a hard life once again. They knew they had entered a different place by a difficult path. The western waters were almost completely separated from the world they had passed through, filled with dangers, and suitable only for those whose character and skills prepared them to persist.

Most of these first migrants into West Virginia were German and Scots-Irish.[1] The former were generally hard-working pacifists who kept to themselves—Lutherans, Quakers, and Dunkard Baptists. The latter preferred to be called Ulster Scots, or simply Scotch, as "nothing sooner offended them than to be called Irish."[2] The Irish were Catholic, of course, but the Scots were Protestant. In the early 1600s their forbears had been transplanted to Ulster, Ireland, from Scotland

---

[1] Otis K. Rice, *The Allegheny Frontier: West Virginia Beginnings, 1730-1830* (Lexington KY: The University Press of Kentucky, 1970), 22; Otis K. Rice, *West Virginia: The State and Its People* (Parsons WV: McClain Printing Company, 1972), 31-32.
[2] Joseph L. Miller, "Our Scotch-Irish Ancestors," *The West Virginia Historical Magazine Quarterly* 3, no.1 (1903): 62-63.

under an ambitious British plan to civilize, dilute, and overwhelm Irish Catholicism and culture. By the turn of the eighteenth century, almost a million Scots lived in Ulster.[3] Unfortunately for the plan, the Scots were largely dissenters who refused to mix with the Catholics *or* bow to the Established Church. Unfortunately for the Scots, the Kingdom and its Church failed to support the massive Ulster enclave to its satisfaction. Rife poverty and famine increased their discontent.

By 1720 the Scots-Irish began immigrating to America. Over the next eighty years, around 250,000 crossed the Atlantic. Searching for religious freedom, economic opportunities, familiar terrain, and kindred spirits, tens of thousands traveled from ports in New Jersey and Delaware through Pennsylvania, where "the presence of the Scotch-Irish was not welcomed. . . . They were regarded as a 'pugnacious' people and undesirable neighbors."[4] So, many continued on and came to rest in the Valley of Virginia, between the Blue Ridge Mountains and the Alleghenies, where the Colony was eager to fortify its western front with migrating colonists. From there, they made their way into West Virginia.

Presbyterian and Appalachian historians present an almost mythic picture of the Scots-Irish. A century of hardship and isolation in Ulster had prepared them for the frontier. They were "a sturdy race, inured to hardships and accustomed to privations."[5] They were independent, hot-headed, industrious, and deeply religious.[6] They were experienced fighters and good marksmen, willing to defend

---

[3] Miller, "Our Scotch-Irish Ancestors," 64.

[4] James R. Graham, *The Planting of the Presbyterian Church in Northern Virginia Prior to the Organization of Winchester Presbytery* (Winchester, VA: Geo. F. Norton Publishing, 1904), 13.

[5] A quote credited to Rev. James Leps of Lewisburg by William T. Price, *Historical Sketch of Greenbrier Presbytery* (Lewisburg, WV: Greenbrier Independent Print., 1889), 17.

[6] Dwight R. Guthrie, *John McMillan, The Apostle of Presbyterianism in the West, 1752-1833* (Pittsburgh: University of Pittsburgh Press, 1952), 3-4.

their lives and lands against savages and tyrants.[7] They were "individualistic and loved democracy,"[8] "insisted on ruling where they lived and made a living,"[9] and "contributed to the formation of the great ideals of liberty."[10] By all accounts, they were perfect for the western waters.

These Protestant Irish were also Presbyterians. It may be an overstatement to say that the Scots-Irish religion united "all their characteristics," but it was true that their creed "thoroughly fired and animated" them.[11] According to the Reverend William T. Price, a Pocahontas County minister, historian, and Confederate chaplain, "their belief in the Divine Sovereignty was such as to imbue them with that unrelenting persistence under difficulties which so eminently prepared for the part they performed in subduing the trackless wilderness and founding new states."[12]

By 1764, the Scots-Irish were "the most numerous...of any denomination in the [Valley of Virginia]."[13] In 1903, the West Virginia Historical Society's magazine opined that "the position of the Scotch-Irish in the New World was peculiar. They alone, of all the various races in America were present in sufficient numbers in all the colonies to make their influence count; and they alone of all the races had one uniform religion."[14] They "brought their Bibles, Catechisms and Confessions of Faith with them; and no sooner was a settlement effected, than measures were taken to provide themselves with the ordinances of religion."[15]

---

[7] *Lexington*, 15; Guthrie, *John McMillan*, 4; Rice, *State*, 32; *Recollections*, 106.
[8] Rice, *State*, 32.
[9] Guthrie, *John McMillan*, 4.
[10] *Lexington*, 12.
[11] Guthrie, *John McMillan*, 4-5.
[12] Price, *Historical Sketch*, 24.
[13] Quoted in Miller, "Our Scotch-Irish Ancestors," 62.
[14] Miller, "Our Scotch-Irish Ancestors," 61.
[15] Graham, *Planting*, 15.

At the 1838 inauguration of the Greenbrier Presbytery, the Reverend Dr. John McElhenney stated that those who first settled the Greenbrier valley "were all inclined to Presbyterianism."[16] He then made the bold claim that "the Presbyterian banner was the first ever set up in this region of the country. So far as is known to us, Presbyterians were the first who preached in these western waters."[17]

———————

Tracing the paths of the settlers explains why the first Presbyterian churches appeared where they did. Identifying the pioneers demonstrates why the population was such a fertile field in which Presbyterianism could take root. Presbyterianism sprouted early, and the first ministers worked like missionaries to grow the fledgling church. But the land of the western waters was not easy to cultivate. Its unique geography made the work exceptionally difficult.

The Reverend McElhenny was one of the earliest, busiest, and most notable pioneers of Presbyterianism in West Virginia. He ministered faithfully for sixty-two years before his passing. His sermon at the Greenbrier's inauguration conveyed both the idyllic and demanding nature of ministry on the western waters:

> Look at the huge mountains which lie in the way, many of which are almost impassable. Look at the bold and rapid streams which pass among them; and bear in mind that not a few of those to whom we are bound to preach the gospel live among the margin of these waters, which are often both difficult and dangerous to cross; and you will see at once that we have undertaken to accomplish a task of no ordinary character.[18]

---

[16] *Recollections*, 237.
[17] *Recollections*, 240. But McElhenney admits here and on p. 249 that the Reverend John Alderson's Baptist church of 1781 may have preceded his.
[18] *Recollections*, 229-30.

3

THE PRINCIPAL CHURCHES

THE MOST OVERARCHING RESOURCE for research on Presbyterian churches in West Virginia is a rare reference work by The Work Projects Administration, called *Inventory of the Church Archives of West Virginia: The Presbyterian Churches.*[1] Created in 1941 as a New Deal project under joint State and Federal sponsorship, the *Inventory* provides a brief historical sketch of every Presbyterian church known to have existed in West Virginia, along with a listing and location for their extant records at the time of publication. Many of these archives are likely untraceable after nearly eighty years. They were in the hands of private individuals who passed long, long ago and have been stored, forgotten, lost, or destroyed by subsequent generations who might not have known their value.

The *Inventory* organizes each church under the headings of presbyteries, synods, and denominations as they existed at the time of the book's creation, even though those structures had already changed many times, and dozens of the listed churches had disappeared long

---

[1] (Charleston, WV: West Virginia Historical Records Survey, 1941). Thanks to Wayne Sparkman of the PCA Historical Center for locating this book, purchasing it, and having it shipped directly to me on the gracious condition that I return it to the PCA archives upon completion of my research.

Table 2 Number of Churches Prior to 1941

Synod/Denomination	Presbytery	Churches	Total
Synod of West Virginia USA	Parkersburg	53	
	Grafton	25	
	Wheeling	31	109
Synod of West Virginia US	Greenbrier	75	
	Kanawha	35	
	Tygart's Valley	5	
	Bluestone	20	135
Synod of Virginia US	Lexington	6	
	Winchester	68	74
		Total Churches	318

before 1941. Regardless, if the *Inventory* is correct, 318 Presbyterian churches have come and gone between 1780 and 1941 (Table 2), a fact that confirms Presbyterianism's former prevalence in the state. Of course, many churches have come and gone since then, but with a focus on early Presbyterianism in West Virginia, this chapter will describe the origins of only a few of the principal churches.

Four Streams

In keeping with West Virginia's "western waters" sobriquet, four separate "streams" of Presbyterianism entered West Virginia, each flowing from separate headwaters, following separate river valleys, and pooling in separate areas of the state. These distinct pockets developed in relative isolation from each at their earliest stages.[2] One stream came from Hanover and Lexington presbyteries down the Greenbrier and

---

[2] The four streams are an organizational pattern suggested by Gill Wilson in his *Story of Presbyterianism in West Virginia* (no publisher, 1958), 15-16. Hereafter, *Story of Presbyterianism*. Wilson deserves credit for recognizing the pattern, even though his book shows problematic signs of being unfinished and is not structured according to his proposal. In spite of its poor state, his is the only book to presents the history of Presbyterianism in West Virginia from the Northern Church perspective.

over to the Kanawha Valley. The Kanawha River led to Point Pleasant on the Ohio River and north to Parkersburg. Another stream came from Connecticut and Massachusetts and travelled up the Tygart River to settle the French Creek area of Upshur County in the north-central portion of the State. A third stream of Presbyterianism came from both Redstone Presbytery and the Covenanter and Seceder denominations in the late 1700s. It followed the Ohio River around the Northern Panhandle and south into the upper Ohio Valley. Redstone also served portions of north-central West Virginia. The fourth stream populated the Northern Neck Proprietary where Winchester Presbytery divided out of Lexington in 1794. Winchester's territory took in the entirety of the Eastern Panhandle.[3]

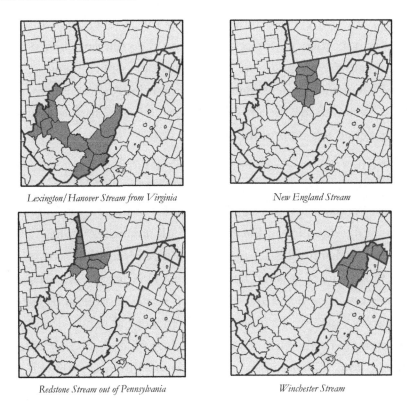

Lexington/Hanover Stream from Virginia

New England Stream

Redstone Stream out of Pennsylvania

Winchester Stream

---

[3] *Story of Presbyterianism*, 27.

The First Churches

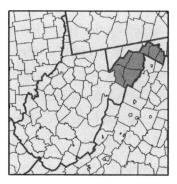

The historian of the Presbytery of Winchester begins his book by boldly claiming that "Presbyterianism in America is autochthonous," by which he means that it grew uniquely and naturally out of American soil and not merely as a European transplant or imitation. It must be acknowledged, however, that Scots-Irish religion enriched the soil in which Presbyterianism took root. Because the pioneers brought their religion with them, "Presbyterians were already there" before the first churches were organized. For this reason, "the early Presbyterian way was the Antioch way: first the congregation, then the preacher. We can date the preacher, but we cannot date the congregation."[4] Historians can assume, therefore, that many "churches" worshiped in West Virginia long before Presbyterian ministers arrived to officially set them in order. The stories of some of the first churches support this assumption.

The first Presbyterian churches in West Virginia were planted east of the Alleghenies along the Northern Neck Proprietary in today's Eastern Panhandle. Once called the Fairfax Grant, this area stretched from the Fairfax Line in the Allegheny Mountains to the headwaters of the Rappahannock River in the Blue Ridge Mountains. The Fairfax Line was a natural western terminus for the Northern Neck because the territory beyond and to the south was rugged, hostile, and generally impassable except by the most experienced and determined adventurers. To the east however, the ruggedness gradually receded into the low rolling hills of the Valley of Virginia, with rich soil,

---

[4] Robert Bell Woodworth, *A History of the Presbytery of Winchester (Synod of Virginia)* (Staunton, VA: McClure Printing Co. 1947), 1-2. Hereafter, *Winchester.*

abundant timber, and large swaths of farmable land.[5] Because of its suitableness and accessibility, this portion of the Valley of Virginia "filled up" long before the path to the western waters opened. It makes sense then that Presbyterian churches would have taken root here first. Between 1720 and 1783, at least ten were planted in the Northern Neck.[6]

People of Potomoke

The first of these ten, and thus the first in West Virginia, may have been in Jefferson County, at the tip of the Eastern Panhandle. In 1719, the Synod of Philadelphia recorded that the "people of Potomoke" (i.e., Potomac) had written to request a minister to "settle among them." The synod responded by sending the Reverend Daniel McGill, who reported back the following year that he had "put the people into church order." The exact location of this church has been debated, although state and presbyterial historians usually claim it was south of the Potomac at or near Shepherdstown.[7] Though the church eventually

---

[5] A long drive down Interstates 68, 64, or 77 will still give visitors a sense of the abrupt transition between the rugged hills of West Virginia (which one must look up at), and the low rolling hills to the east (which one can look out upon). The transition to the open vistas of Maryland and Virginia is breathtaking! Even today the drive demonstrates what the early West Virginia settlers were up against as they traveled west.

[6] According to the *Inventory* (269), these churches were at Shepherdstown (1720), Summit Point (1740), Hedgesville (1740), Tuscarora Creek (1740), Spring Mills (1745), Smithfield (1773), Fort Ashby (1782), Romney (1782), Springfield (1782), and Gerrardstown (1783).

[7] Graham, *Planting*, 7; Rice and Brown, *West Virginia: A History*, 14; Rice, *The Allegheny Frontier*, 18; Rice, *State*, 27. Graham argues that the Potomoke congregation continued under different names until it eventually became the Elk Branch Presbyterian Church in 1769. Woodworth, on the other hand, did not believe this church to be located in West Virginia at all. He placed it "near Chesapeake Bay between the Rappahannock and Potomac rivers, somewhere east of Potomac Creek" (*Winchester*, 6, 57). He does suggest that the Shepherdstown church was at least related to the early Potomoke congregation by division, however (7). The most thorough discussion of all the options appears to be by Dorsey Ellis in *Look unto the Rock* (Parsons WV: McClain Printing Company, 1982), 328-345. He concludes that it was at or near Shepherdstown.

disappeared from record, its existence is of significant interest beyond church history. A permanent settlement there in 1719 would have been the first west of the Blue Ridge, an exciting possibility for both West Virginia and Virginia historians. But other than this reference to a church whose location is uncertain, no other record of a settlement exists. Instead, historians place the first settlements after 1730 when Virginia Council land grants commenced.[8] Perhaps the people of Potomoke were early squatters, but much about the congregation remains a mystery. Nonetheless, it certainly existed, and it has been granted "first church" status by the Presbyterians of West Virginia.

New Lebanon ARP

The Old Stone Church of Lewisburg is popularly thought to be the oldest Presbyterian church on the western waters, organized in 1783.[9] But the honor of "first church west of the Alleghenies" probably goes instead to an Associate Reformed Church in Monroe County, about fifteen miles south of Lewisburg—New Lebanon Presbyterian Church of Pickaway, in an area originally known simply as "the Sink-hole lands." The origin story of this "Sinks" church is murky, but it is possible that Presbyterians in both Greenbrier and Monroe counties were meeting for worship without regular supply as far back as 1772. A disagreement seems to have arisen, perhaps over music, and the

---

[8] Rice, *The Allegheny Frontier*, 18. James R. Graham made a case in 1904 for a settlement at or near Shepherdstown as early as 1707 (*Planting*, 7). But his case depends in part upon an illegible death date on a mysterious German grave marker. The fascinating story of this tombstone and a strong refutation that it proves an early settlement is found in Stephen Stec, "Catarina Beierlin's Gravestone Revisited," *The Magazine of the Jefferson County Historical Society* 82 (December 2016): 17-32. The original tombstone is housed in the West Virginia Archives in Charleston. It is worth mentioning because it was once accepted and still occasionally surfaces as "proof" of West Virginia's first legendary settlement.

[9] See, for instance, *Greenbrier*, 60; *Story of Presbyterianism*, 17; *Recollections*, 238-39; and Howard McKnight Wilson, *The Lexington Presbytery Heritage: The Presbytery of Lexington and Its Churches in the Synod of Virginia Presbyterian Church in the United States, 1786-1970* (Verona, VA: McClure Press, 1971), 101. Hereafter, *Lexington*.

New Lebanon ARP Church in Monroe County is probably the oldest Presbyterian Church in Trans-Allegheny West Virginia. The current building was built in the early 1870, although the congregation had been meeting since the 1770s.

Sinks portion divided out to form its own congregation. In 1777 they appealed to Hanover and Lexington for pulpit supply, as well as to the Associate Reformed Church (a separated Covenanter and Seceder denomination out of Pennsylvania). When the latter was the only one to respond in a timely fashion, the Sinks congregation—now named New Lebanon—officially became Associate Reformed.[10] Lewisburg's John McElhenney "frequently preached in the Seceders' church, as that congregation had considerable periods in its own history during which it had the services of no one of its own ministry."[11] As a member of a separate denomination, New Lebanon remained segregated from

---

[10] Local Monroe County historian James W. Banks presents details the origins of New Lebanon Presbyterian Church in *200 Years from Good Hope* (Parsons, WV: McClain Print., 1983), 24-25. A phone call to the most recent pastor confirms that the location of the church's records from this period are unknown.

[11] *Recollections*, 92.

most mainline goings-on in the decades that followed. It still exists as a small, conservative Associate Reformed Presbyterian (ARP) church in Sinks Grove, West Virginia. Other sources including the Reverend McElhenney confirm that it was there at the beginning of Presbyterianism on the western waters.[12] Thus it must be the first Presbyterian church west of the Alleghenies.

Three Cornerstone Churches

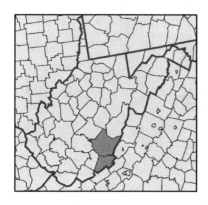

The Lewisburg or "Old Stone" church followed soon after. In 1783, Hanover Presbytery of Virginia commissioned the Reverend John McCue (1753-1818), "the first resident Presbyterian Minister west of the Alleghenies," to preach to the Presbyterian settlers on the western waters.[13] He founded three churches informally referred to as "the Cornerstone Churches," because "it was from these congregations that the impulse was given to Presbyterianism in this whole western region of Virginia."[14]

Lewisburg

The first of the Cornerstone Churches was the Old Stone Church of Lewisburg. The congregation first met in 1783 in a log building "in the midst of a large field some one and one-half miles northwest" of town.[15] Originally it was called the "Camp Union Church," after the military camp that predated Lewisburg. (It was also sometimes called by what appears to have been the malapropism "Companion

---

[12] *Recollections*, 257-59. See also Banks, *200 Years*, 24-25; *Inventory*, 107-8.
[13] *Greenbrier*, 60.
[14] *Recollections*, 259.
[15] John Fleshman Montgomery, *History of the Old Stone Presbyterian Church 1783-1983* (Parsons, WV: McClain Printing Company, 1983), 7.

The Rehoboth Methodist Church in Monroe County is an example of a frontier log meeting house. It is the oldest extant church structure west of the Alleghenies, though it is no longer used for worship. The roof is a pavilion that protects the original structure.

Church.")[16] In 1796, the church constructed a stone meeting house and took the name "Lewisburg Presbyterian Church." Over the decades the stone building became an icon of the community. By the early twentieth century the church was known to all simply as "The Old Stone Church," though the name was not made official until 1920.[17]

Union and Spring Creek

The Reverend McCue also founded two other nearby churches at about the same time: Union Church (known first as Peace, then Good Hope, Concord, and finally Union) was 20 miles to the south in Monroe County, and Spring Creek Church in Renick was sixteen miles to the north.[18] For around seven years, he pastored all three through what appears to have been a joint call from the Lewisburg and Union

---

[16] This is nowhere explained to be a malapropism but seems a reasonable conjecture.

[17] Montgomery, *History of the Old Stone Presbyterian Church*, 9.

[18] See Banks, *200 Years,* for the stories of Union and other churches in what is now Monroe County.

This stone is an azimuth marker for the original log meeting house of the Lewisburg Presbyterian Church (1783-1796). Located on the Tuckwiller farm about five miles west of town, it was "560 feet south" beyond the point of the stone. Dissenter congregations originally built outside of towns to minimize regulation problems and religious conflicts. Thanks to Mr. Sam Tuckwiller for inviting me onto the property and giving me a tour.

churches and as the occasional supply of the Spring Creek Church.[19] In 1794, after a three year vacancy, the Reverend Benjamin Grigsby (1770-1810) was installed to the same arrangement by the Lexington Presbytery, which had been birthed from Hanover in 1786. It was under Grigsby's tenure that the historic stone meeting house was built, along with a similarly constructed stone manse that still stands in Caldwell on the Greenbrier River.[20] In 1808, the Lewisburg and Union

---

[19] Montgomery, *History of the Old Stone Presbyterian Church*, 33. McElhenney called the Lewisburg and Union churches "united congregations" in *Recollections*, 154.

[20] The church is located at the corner of Church Street and West Foster in Lewisburg. Both the church and manse are listed with the National Register of Historic Places. Still in use as a residence, the manse is located on Stone House Road north of Caldwell, shortly after the road turns sharply away from the Greenbrier River (pictured on p. 60). The family retained the house after Grigsby left in 1801 and did not sell it until 1842. The next pastor, McElhenney, built his

The Old Stone Church and Cemetery pictured from the southeast.

Churches initiated the sixty-year pastorate of the Reverend Dr. John McElhenney (1781-1871) whose life and ministry factor strongly in the history of West Virginia Presbyterianism. Though they are small and their original meeting houses are long gone, the Union and Spring Creek churches still meet today.

The Old Stone Church has always been the largest and most notable of the three Cornerstone Churches. It may not have been the first transmontane church, but it was among the first, and the congregation has the honor of meeting in the oldest church building "still in continuous use" west of the Alleghenies. The church was built in 1796 with the generous support of Colonel John Stuart. He and his wife Agatha donated the land and 650 pounds toward its construction. Colonel Stuart (1749-1823) was an early West Virginia pioneer, wealthy businessman and landowner, participant in the Battle of Point

own brick house closer to the Old Stone Church, because the manse was privately owned and "was located nearly five miles from the Old Stone Church and approximately twenty miles from Good Hope [Union Church]."

Pleasant, cousin to the famed Colonel Andrew Lewis (after whom Lewisburg was named), and elder of the Old Stone Church.[21] It is said that he himself cut the inscription in the sandstone rock still embedded above the church door, now weathered and barely legible:

THIS
BUILDING WAS
ERRECTED IN THE YEAR
1796 AT THE EXPENCE
OF A FEW OF THE FIRST
INHABITANTS OF THIS
LAND TO COMMEMORATE
THEIR AFFECTION &
ESTEEM FOR THE
HOLY GOSPEL OF
JESUS CHRIST

READER,
IF YOU ARE INCLINED
TO APPLAUD THEIR
VIRTUES GIVE
GOD THE GLORY

---

[21] The church's historian supposed that Stuart was an elder, although the church has no record of this (Montgomery, *History of the Old Stone Presbyterian Church*, 203). It is certain that he was a member.

The weather-worn stone above the entrance. The location of the stone can be seen in the picture on the front cover.

All three churches struggled in their early years. Presbyterianism may have laid first claim to the western waters, but by the time the Reverend John McElhenny was installed in 1808, the once healthy churches had lost many members. This has been blamed on factors like the rowdiness of camp life during the war and the constant westward flow of migration: "During this troublesome time, the ranks of the church were being steadily depleted as families moved on to the west, to the Ohio and Kentucky, and southward to Tennessee."[22] McElhenney blamed the poor state in which he found the churches on the long pulpit vacancies between McCue and Grigsby (three years) and between Grigsby and himself (seven years). Without regular supply, defections—regardless of prior theological conviction—were inevitable. Some Presbyterians would "lay aside their differences and their strong

---

[22] Banks, *200 Years*, 28, 38.

Scots-Irish Presbyterian heritage to embrace the Methodist and Baptist faiths. Heritage was one thing, availability was something else."[23]

McElhenney adjudged that the Presbyterian method of supplying churches was simply not as suited to the frontier as were other systems. When he preached his semi-centenary sermon in 1858, he stated that the Union and Lewisburg had only "between forty and fifty" members when he arrived. By that time, other denominations, though later on the scene, were already surpassing the work of the Lexington Presbytery: "There were, at the commencement of this period of fifty years, 169 members in the Baptist Church in Greenbrier.... in the Methodist Episcopal Church, in the whole circuit, 504 members.... In the Associate Reformed Church in Monroe 120." He acknowledged that Presbyterianism had fallen behind, and for valid reasons, but he was not discouraged:

> Presbyterianism has labored under peculiar disadvantages. That congregations may be gathered and pastors settled, a compact population is required; and this never has yet existed, except in a few limited sections of the territory covered by the Greenbrier Presbytery. The greater part of the population is scattered along the creeks and rivers which wind their way among lofty mountains and steep hills. To reach these sparse settlements requires much laborious travelling on horseback; so that the itinerant system [i.e., Methodism] is much better adapted to a large portion of this region than the Presbyterian plan of settled pastors. In looking over the ground, there is not more cause for humiliation that so little has been done than there is for gratitude that so much has been accomplished in circumstances so disadvantageous.[24]

When McElhenney arrived as pastor in 1808, the three Cornerstone Churches were the only Presbyterian congregations on

---

[23] Banks, *200 Years*, 38. *Recollections* records McElhenney's description of the dire condition of the Cornerstone churches upon his arrival in 1808 (239).
[24] *Recollections*, 259-260.

the western waters.[25] Until 1818, he himself was the only ordained Presbyterian minister between Lewisburg and the Ohio River. His reputation for diligence and his longevity in ministry gave him an unusual influence throughout this vast territory.[26] Not only did McElhenney pastor these three churches, but he has been credited with starting nearly a dozen more at great distances.[27] By the time the territory was ready to have its own presbytery in 1838, the number of churches had grown to fourteen or fifteen, mostly due to McElhenney's tireless itineration and leadership. As the ministers of the new Greenbrier presbytery met together for the first time in Lewisburg, McElhenney told them,

> There are, at this time, in this presbytery, fifteen congregations; nine of these lie immediately on or near to the Greenbrier River; one in Kanawha County; one at Point Pleasant; one in Parkersburg, in the county of Wood; another in a remote part of that county; one in French Creek, in Lewis County; and one in the county of Randolph; containing in all from twelve to fifteen hundred members.[28]

McElhenney's list does not account for the planting of churches in West Virginia by other presbyteries outside Greenbrier's boundaries during the same period. Between the years of 1787 and 1838, Redstone organized at least eight churches in the Northern Panhandle and seven in the north-central portion of the state (e.g., Morgantown, Clarksburg,

---

[25] Since it was a different denomination, the Associate Reformed congregation in Monroe County was generally ignored in early mainline discussions.

[26] *Greenbrier*, 24

[27] Viz., Summersville, Muddy Creek, Anthony's Creek, Carmel at Gap Mills, Frankford, Mount Pleasant, McElhenney Church at Grassy Meadows, Salem, and others. Compiled from respective sections in *Greenbrier*.

[28] *Recollections*, 240. Other more specific lists contain only fourteen churches, viz., Lewisburg, Union, Spring Creek, Oak Grove, Head of Greenbrier (now Liberty), Tygart's Valley, Anthony's Creek, Parkersburg, Point Pleasant, Hughes River, Carmel, Huttonsville, Charleston, and Muddy Creek" (*Greenbrier*, 15; see also *Lexington*, 102). Perhaps McElhenney includes a mission congregation.

and Fairmont).[29] The Associate Reformed Church also planted at least one in Wheeling (United in 1833). Both areas were accessible by the Ohio and Monongahela Rivers long before the remote interior of Greenbrier's territory. Still, Greenbrier Presbytery bore responsibility for the largest swath of rugged terrain across the middle of the state.

Three Kanawha Valley Churches

Three historic Presbyterian churches in the Kanawha Valley of West Virginia mark 2019 as their bicentennial. Though all three claim to have originated in 1819, each has a different organization date spanning fifty years. How then can all three celebrate the same bicentennial? And which church is truly the original?

Kanawha and Kanawha Salines

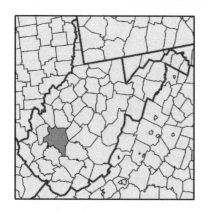

Their story actually begins a few years earlier, in 1815, when the wealthy Ruffner family built a 200-seat meeting house on their Malden property for use by the *Society of Christians Called Presbyterians.*[30] At about the same time, the family also donated another plot of their land five

---

[29] In the northern panhandle, these were Forks of Wheeling (1787), West Liberty (1788), Fairview of Pughtown (1793), Tent United of Follansbee (1798), First of Wheeling (1828), Wolf Run of Cameron (1829), West Union of Dallas (1831), and First of Moundsville (1835); In north-central West Virginia were First of Morgantown (1788), First of Fairmont (1815), French Creek of Upshur County (1819), First of Clarksburg (1839), Brown's of Stewartstown (1834), Sugar Grove of Laurel Point (1835), and Kingwood (1837). Compiled from *Inventory,* s.v.

[30] *Kanawha,* 71. Early Presbyterians used the terms "society" and "meeting house" instead of "church" and "sanctuary" because of the presbyterian conviction that churches should be properly organized by ordained ministers who could regularly preach and administer the sacraments. The terms were also likely carried over from the colonial era when dissenting churches were highly regulated. A society in a meeting house was less subject to regulation than a church in a sanctuary. The

miles to the north in Charleston, stipulating "one moiety for education, one moiety for the *Society of Christians Called Presbyterians*."[31] On March 14, 1819, one of the Ruffner boys, Henry, having been freshly ordained by Lexington Presbytery, organized this group as a single church meeting in two locations—one in Charleston and the other in Malden. It was known simply as "the Church on Kanawha in Charleston and at Kanawha Salines."

After Ruffner immediately left to assume an academic post at Washington College in Lexington, the two united congregations hired Congregationalist Calvin Chaddock, a Boston minister who died in the Kanawha Valley after only a few short years on the job. Next was Nathaniel Calhoon, a minister and medical doctor with whom the congregation quickly became dissatisfied for some unknown reason. Then in 1837 came the Reverend James Moore Brown who ministered in the Valley for twenty-five years. Each of these preached at both locations five miles apart on designated Sundays.

On the plot in Charleston, the church first built the Mercer Academy, in which the Charleston congregation met for many years. The Malden congregation worshiped at "Colonel Ruffner's Meeting House" until the late 1830s, when the family donated more land in Malden for the construction of the permanent brick sanctuary in which the congregation still meets today. Shortly after, in 1841, Reverend Brown led the Malden congregation to divide out and organize as the "Kanawha Salines Church." This new church called the Reverend Stuart Robinson as its first pastor, and James Moore Brown preached his installation service. Reverend Brown continued as the pastor of the original "Kanawha Church" in Charleston until his death in 1862.

Ruffners believed any Christianity was better than none, so the meeting house "at the mouth of Georges Creek" was used by other denominations also.
[31] *Kanawha*, 71.

The Kanawha Salines Presbyterian Church sometime in the nineteenth century; picture courtesy of the church.

The Kanawha Salines Presbyterian Church today. Established in 1841.

First Presbyterian of Charleston

Still a third church traces its origin to 1819—ironically called the "First" Presbyterian Church of Charleston. It was actually organized in 1872 when a majority of the Kanawha Church decided they wanted to adhere to the Southern Church. A vote was taken, the church divided, and the two congregations split the property. The new "Presbyterian Church of Charleston" (later to add the word "First") continued with the Southern PCUS. The Kanawha Presbyterian Church joined the Northern PCUSA.

So, which of the three was first? While all three can legitimately trace their histories to Henry Ruffner and to that March 14th date in 1819, the Kanawha Church technically has the best claim to being the mother congregation. It birthed the Kanawha Salines Church in 1841 and the First Presbyterian Church in 1872. The order of the former is settled by the Kanawha Church's minutes of September 1, 1841: "Resolved, that Greenbrier Presbytery be requested to divide the Kanawha Church by constituting a church to be known by the name of Kanawha Salines Church."[32] The order of the latter is settled not only by its clear date of organization thirty years later, but by the awarding of the minute books to the Kanawha Church by the secular courts, thus certifying it as the continuing congregation, at least in the eyes of the state. The seeds of all three, however, were indubitably contained within the original congregations that were organized in 1819.

So, in spite of organization dates that span fifty years, all three can— at least in spirit—claim a 2019 bicentennial. The Kanawha Church— now known as the Kanawha United Presbyterian Church—stands only a few short blocks from its younger sister, the First Presbyterian Church. As sibling PC(USA) congregations, they have long since "made up." The historic Kanawha Salines Presbyterian Church in Malden joined the dissident Vanguard Presbytery in 1972 and became a charter member of the Presbyterian Church in America in 1973.

---

[32] Photocopies of the minutes are held by the Kanawha Salines Church.

Three Ohio Valley Churches

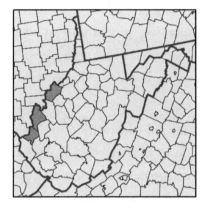

Several West Virginia churches on the Ohio River got their start through the efforts of ministers from Ohio. Because the Trans-Allegheny terrain was so rough, the rivers were major travel arteries that carried settlers into the Ohio Valley quite early in West Virginia's history. Settlements tended to grow up around the mouths of tributaries because these "western waters" allowed traffic to push through or around the denser, more mountainous regions and left a frontier-like gap between the Ohio and the Alleghenies. Even though ministers were organizing churches in the Kanawha Valley in the early 1800s, settlers in the Parkersburg, Point Pleasant, and Huntington areas were often evangelized by ministers from across the river, in the quickly-developing territory of Ohio.

Point Pleasant

Settlers arrived early in Point Pleasant because of its strategic location at the confluence of the Kanawha and Ohio Rivers. Known today for its Mothman legend and the 1967 Silver Bridge collapse, the town's greatest historical significance lies in the 1774 Battle of Point Pleasant. Several later members of the Lewisburg Presbyterian Church fought there, including Colonel John Stuart.[33]

---

[33] Colonel John Stuart wrote a first-person account of the Battle of Point Pleasant, the only battle of Lord Dunmore's War. Lord Dunmore, governor of the Colony of Virginia, wanted to put an end to Indian skirmishes on the colony's western borders. He ordered Andrew Lewis at Camp Union (Lewisburg, WV) to set out for Point Pleasant with his 800 troops, while he set out from Pittsburgh with his 1,700. The two armies would meet to attack Chief Cornstalk's Shawnee warriors together. On his way south along the Ohio, Dunmore camped above Saint Marys, missing

The Point Pleasant Church began as an offshoot of a congregation across the river in Gallipolis, Ohio. Their pastor, Rev. William Gould, a Congregationalist educated at Yale and Andover, began preaching additional services in Point Pleasant in 1815.[34] By 1835, the Lexington Presbytery was ready to take the new congregation under its own care and sent Rev. Francis Dutton to be its first pastor.[35] Point Pleasant became one of the founding churches of the Greenbrier Presbytery but split in the wake of the Civil War, a story which will be told later.

Parkersburg

Fifty miles up the river from Point Pleasant was the town of Parkersburg, at the mouth of what is known as the Little Kanawha River. The church there was organized in 1833 by James McAboy, another Ohio minister. McAboy had started out as the pastor of a local Baptist church, but the Ohio presbytery ordained him in 1830. Several Presbyterian families had already established themselves in Parkersburg, and after hearing some of McAboy's revival preaching

his appointment with Lewis and leaving Lewis to be ambushed by the Shawnee at Point Pleasant. Many died on both sides, including Lewis's brother, Charles. Though the Shawnee army was larger, the colonists won, Cornstalk's army retreated, and Lewis pursued. By the time he caught up with them deep in Ohio territory, Dunmore had already negotiated a treaty with Cornstalk. Stuart recounted that Lewis always suspected Dunmore intentionally missed the meet-up. It has been supposed his goal was to weaken the western front's fighting stock in view of the impending revolution. The Battle of Point Pleasant further prepared Indian territory for colonial expansion, and suspicions of treachery may have catalyzed Trans-Allegheny participation in the Revolution. See John Stuart, "Memorandum—1798, July 15th," *The West Virginia Historical Magazine Quarterly* 5, no. 2 (1905): 127-132.

[34] *Inventory*, 155; *Story of Presbyterianism*, 71; *Kanawha*, 353-370.
[35] "Dutton was born in Massachusetts, June 28, 1790; educated at Princeton University and Washington College, served as a tutor at Washington College, and as instructor in military school, at Staunton; and principal of Lewisburg Academy; licensed 1834 by Greenbrier Presbytery [*sic*—Lexington?]; died 1850, while serving the Point Pleasant Church, and is buried in the Pioneer Cemetery" (*Inventory*, 155). Dutton also founded the Buffalo Presbyterian Church about twenty miles up the Kanawha River.

in 1832, they petitioned Lexington to organize them as a church. Nathan Calhoon and one of his elders came up from Kanawha to make it official.[36]

Like Point Pleasant, the Parkersburg Church was one of the founding churches of the Greenbrier Presbytery, but it departed in 1863 when the Northern Assembly tried to dissolve Greenbrier and Lexington Presbyteries and replace them with the Presbytery of West Virginia—yet another story that will be told later.[37] Its preeminence in the Northern Church is illustrated by the fact that the first meeting of that new Northern presbytery was held in Parkersburg, and that when the time came to change the presbytery's name in 1892, the Northern Church called it the "Presbytery of Parkersburg."

Huntington

Situated forty miles south of Point Pleasant, Huntington is another town that was established near the mouth of a tributary— the tiny Guyandotte River. The First Presbyterian Church of Huntington got its start in 1838 by Guyandotte residents who grew weary of rowing across the river to attend worship at the log church in Burlington every week:

> Before the organization of the Huntington Church, the Presbyterian farmers of Cabell County went in boats with their families across the river to Burlington to worship. It was practically an all day trip; and it was necessary to row or sometimes push the boats across the river. Sometimes the pastor came to Huntington and the services were conducted in a barn, or in a home, or in the open woods.[38]

---

[36] *Inventory*, 25; *Story of Presbyterianism*, 19-20.
[37] *Greenbrier*, 28.
[38] *Kanawha*, 378. Organized in 1786, the Burlington Church was across the Ohio River and five miles to west. The river could be waded in places because it was

The Presbyterians of Guyandotte saw their chance to have their own church when the surrounding community started making plans for an academy near the Guyandotte River. In order to secure a meeting place, they committed to generously supporting the construction of the new school's facilities. The Methodists apparently made the same arrangement, so for the next quarter century they alternated services, perhaps even meeting jointly, in Marshall Academy's chapel. When the academy fell into private hands during the war, the Methodists and Presbyterians continued sharing preachers and eventually went together on the construction of a shared building.[39]

This "Guyandotte Church" started out in Abingdon Presbytery but petitioned to join the Greenbrier in September of 1838. The Greenbrier simply recorded it as "the Western Church" because it immediately became (and remained) the Presbytery's westernmost congregation.[40] The church elected Rev. Alfred Thom as its first pastor. He had formerly pastored the Burlington church, and circumstances suggest that his eagerness to take the new position may have been due in part to his owning a "slave girl" named Susie, which was illegal on the Ohio side. Thom baptized Susie into membership on March 15, 1841—"one of the few instances in West Virginia history where a Christian preacher administered the rite of baptism to his own slave."[41]

---

significantly smaller and shallower prior to construction of nineteen locks and dams.

[39] *Kanawha*, 381.

[40] *Inventory*, 157.

[41] *Kanawha*, 380. This claim might be overstated. Many early Presbyterian ministers owned slaves, had concern for their religion, and would have baptized them when appropriate. See *Inventory* (157) for the suggestion that Thom had ulterior motives for the move.

Three North-Central Churches

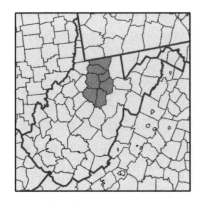 Presbyterian societies had been meeting for worship in the north-central part of the state as early as 1788. Braddock's Road had initially led settlers to the Pittsburgh area from where they naturally overflowed to the south, up the Monongahela River, and into the various tributaries that form its watershed. Churches there developed in isolation from the rest of the state, mainly under the care of Redstone Presbytery. Many of them had strong ties to New England where Congregationalist influences ran strong.

French Creek

Monongalia through Upshur Counties, especially, received an influx of Congregationalist and Presbyterian settlers from Massachusetts and Connecticut around the turn of the nineteenth century. They met regularly for worship, read published sermons, and prayed for ministers to provide the ordinances of worship. For a while, the answer to those prayers came in occasional supply from Redstone. Sources also mention a Congregationalist missionary from New England by the name of Aretas Loomis (1790-1856) as "the first man to give Presbyterianism an aggressive form in Tygart's Valley."[42] Then in 1816, the Congregationalist Central Association of Hampshire County, Massachusetts, sent the newly ordained Asa Brooks (c. 1790-1834) as a missionary to northern West Virginia. His commission read as follows:

---

[42] *Greenbrier*, 38; *Story of Presbyterianism*, 23. See also Elisha Scott Loomis, *Descendants of Joseph Loomis in America: And His Antecedents in the Old World* (Self-published, 1909), 195.

We the Trustees of the Hampshire Missionary Society, do by these presents, appoint and constitute you, the said Rev. Asa Brooks, of Buckhannon, in the county of Lewis, Commonwealth of Virginia, a Missionary of the Cross of Christ, under the authority of said Society. . . to perform the customary labours of a Missionary in the towns and each settlement which are in the vicinity of Buckhannon and French crick, and which are most destitute and which are now ready to receive your [ministry]. In your zeal and constancy and in your ability to discharge well that sacred trust under the guidance of the Holy Spirit, we repose full confidence. Of you we expect and require that, with all due diligence and fidelity, you perform the work of an Evangelist by dispensing the pure doctrines to the people to whom you are sent, and in the establishment and consolation of his saints. As you have strength and opportunity, dispense the gospel and its ordinances upon the Lord's Day and other days; visit schools and instruct children; administer Christian Light and consolation to the sick and dying; comfort those who mourn. Be it your great labor and matter of your fervent supplications that you may be the instrument of bringing home souls to the Shepherd and Bishop of souls. Be a good steward of the mysteries of God. Faithfully keep the trust which we commit to you as becometh that servant who expects to give an account of his stewardship at the Great Day.[43]

Brooks set about preaching throughout his assigned territory, but his first plant was the French Creek Church, about ten miles south of Buckhannon. The *Inventory of the Church Archives of West Virginia* records their first sessional entry in 1819:

French Creek, Lewis Virginia. There being in this settlement a number, both male and female, having letters of recommendation from different Congregational Churches in Mass. with which they were united previous to their emigrating to this place, and wishing again to be favored with church privileges, a time was publically appointed for the election of Ruling Elders.'[44]

---

[43] Quoted in *Inventory*, 60-61. Edited for sense and punctuation.
[44] *Inventory*, 61.

French Creek promptly called Brooks to be their first pastor. As he had transferred his credentials to Redstone sometime in the previous three years, the new congregation was officially a Presbyterian church. No doubt influenced by its Congregationalist heritage, it was also one of several north and north-central congregations that chose to affiliate with Northern Church when it started the Presbytery of West Virginia in 1863. Later, Dr. Loyal Young—the very man who had spawned the Presbytery of West Virginia through his motion to the General Assembly—became the pastor of this congregation and at Buckhannon from 1868-1875.[45]

Clarksburg

The diligent and productive Rev. Asa Brooks also founded the Clarksburg Church ten years after French Creek. Situated about forty-five miles to the north, Clarksburg was a bustling town of about 700 people in a growing county of 15,000.[46] Brooks had been travelling, preaching, and tending flocks throughout the region for years, as was the habit of ministers where supply was wanting. By 1829, his Clarksburg flock was ready to organize. The church's first minute book opens with the following:

> Whereas the Rev. Asa Brooks of the Congregation of French Creek and of the Presbyterian Church within the bounds of the Red Stone Presbytery…duly authorized to preach the Gospel, administer the ordinances and establish churches within said bounds, together with David Phillips, Roswell Knowlton, and Pascal Young ruling Elders of the French Creek Church, on the 10th day of October, 1829 at the Methodist Meeting House in Clarksburg did proceed to establish a Presbyterian Church in the said Town of Clarksburg.[47]

---

[45] *Story of Presbyterianism*, 29.
[46] *Story of Presbyterianism*, 97.
[47] In possession of the First Presbyterian Church of Clarksburg and on display in the lobby.

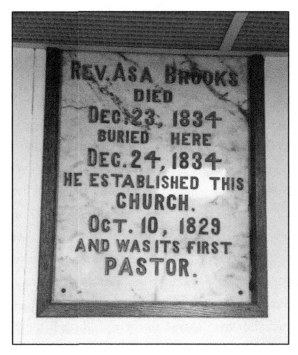

Asa Brooks' final resting place in the basement wall and under the pulpit of the First Presbyterian Church of Clarksburg.

Brooks became the first stated supply, and two years later, he moved with his wife and eight children to Clarksburg to become their first pastor, while remaining the occasional supply of the French Creek Church.

After having ministered in this area and to these people for almost twenty years, Brooks passed away of "bilious fever" in December of 1834. He was forty-four years of age. The church had started construction of a building the previous July and buried Mr. Brooks under the pulpit—it has been said—"so that the church would never be without a pastor."[48] Mr. Brooks reposed there until 1889. When age made that structure no longer safe for meetings (which had the added benefit—it has also been said—of shortening sermons), the church built another sanctuary nearby and

---

[48] Though entrenched in the church's history, I have not encountered a primary source for this quote. See "The History of First Presbyterian Church Clarksburg WV," accessed March 7, 2019, www.clarksburgfpc.org.

promptly reinterred Brooks under the pulpit once again. The original marble slab still marks his tomb in the basement walls.

Morgantown

The Presbyterians that settled the Morgantown area were from purer Presbyterian stock than other parts of north-central West Virginia, though they were still of northern origin—perhaps from New York and Pennsylvania. Redstone sent Rev. Robert Finley to do the first missionary work and organize the Morgantown church in 1788, followed by Rev. Joseph Patterson as their first pastor. They met at the courthouse for nearly thirty years, until they and the Episcopalians joined to build a shared sanctuary on the "Sepulchre Lot" in 1818. The Virginia Assembly had set this lot aside for religious use under the local governance of trustees, comprising seven Presbyterians and two Episcopalians. Wilson calls their first house of worship the "Union Church," although the two groups remained distinct.[49]

The reader will later learn that Presbyterianism struggled in comparison to other denominations in West Virginia. In this case for once—in the disestablishment soil of the western waters—Episcopalianism did not thrive nearly as well as Presbyterianism. Their branch of the partnership was too weak to even support a minister, much more to contribute to renovations or construction. Over time, use and care of the property devolved to the Presbyterians alone. So, when the Presbyterians unilaterally built a new house of worship on the property after the Civil War, and when the Episcopalians reasserted their original claim to the property by virtue of the original public trust, "the matter had to be settled by the Court, which ruled that, by right of use for fifty years, the Presbyterians owned the building."[50] Like the French Creek and Clarksburg congregations, the Morgantown

---

[49] *Inventory*, 57-58; *Story of Presbyterianism*, 94.
[50] *Story of Presbyterianism*, 95.

Presbyterians joined the Northern Church's Presbytery of West Virginia during the Civil War. Two hundred years later, the First Presbyterian Church still sits on that same Sepulchre Lot on the corner of Spruce Street and Forest Avenue in the heart of Morgantown.

4

PRESBYTERIES, SYNODS, AND DENOMINATIONS

THE CHIEF DISTINCTIVE OF Presbyterianism is not infant baptism, Covenant theology, or Reformed doctrine, though all these typically come with the package. The defining characteristic of Presbyterianism is its specific form of connectionalism: "The Church is one in such a sense that a smaller part is subject to a larger, and the larger to the whole. It has one Lord, one faith, one baptism"; and "during the apostolic age the churches were not independent bodies, but subject in all matters of doctrine, order, and discipline to a common tribunal."[1] From smaller to larger, these tribunals are sessions, presbyteries, synods, and assemblies. As presbyteries join with others to form synods and general assemblies, the church visibly manifests the spiritual unity of the Body of Christ. Consistent with this conviction, the first Presbyterians in West Virginia set out to form their own denominational structures as soon as possible.

Over the course of two centuries, these structures and boundaries changed in ways that are difficult to trace. Few narratives of the whole

---

[1] Charles Hodge, *What Is Presbyterianism* (Philadelphia: Presbyterian Board of Education, 1855), 75-76. For a more recent discussion of Presbyterian connectionalism see my *A Church You Can See: Building a Case for Church Membership* (New Martinsville WV: ReformingWV Publications, 2017), 30-35, as well as its defense of denominationalism (77-86).

exist, since presbyteries and churches mostly recorded only their own histories. Those histories that do venture outside their own borders are sometimes muddled with minute details about normal restructurings, boundary adjustments, conflicts, divisions, excisions, and secessions. Instead of getting bogged down in details, this chapter seeks to draw the largest possible picture of presbytery development in West Virginia, using only the broadest strokes. Thus, it omits less consequential developments. Even so, the big picture is still difficult to take in (hence the visual aid of Figure 1).

In 1755, the Synod of New York established the Presbytery of Hanover to encompass the Colony of Virginia, including the unsettled western waters of Trans-Allegheny Virginia. In 1781, four ministers of western Pennsylvania were established as the Redstone Presbytery, which included what would later become north-central West Virginia and the Northern Panhandle.[2] With its residual New Side inclinations, Hanover maintained "an aggressive program of evangelism" in the Shenandoah Valley, eventually reaching across the Alleghenies with the commissioning of John McCue in 1782.[3] Near Lewisburg, he established the three Cornerstone Churches in 1783.

As the Scots-Irish community increased west of the Blue Ridge Mountains, and as the number of Presbyterian ministers there (twelve) surpassed the number to the east (eight), Hanover saw the need to divide out additional presbyteries. The time was right because the denomination was restructuring itself with the goal of bringing a variety of newly created synods under the authority of a single General Assembly.[4] In 1785, the Synod of New York and Philadelphia (which had previously joined in the Old-Side/New Side reconciliation of

---

[2] Andrew G. Slade, *Presbyterianism in the Upper Ohio Valley* (Steubenville OH: Presbytery of the Upper Ohio Valley, 1976), 4.
[3] *Lexington*, 44; *Greenbrier*, 21.
[4] *Lexington*, 65-66.

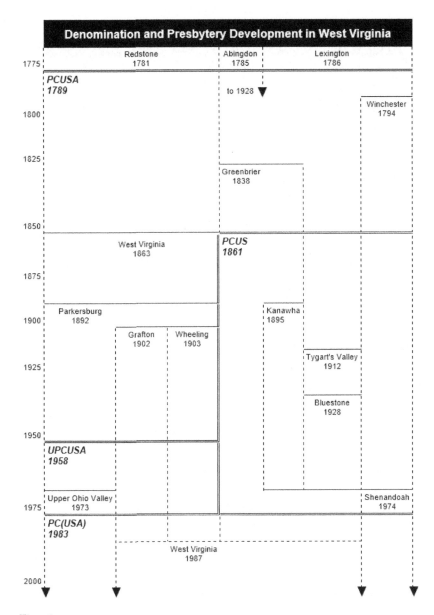

Figure 1

1758) created Abingdon Presbytery (with all of three its ministers) to serve the territory that extended southwest of the Kanawha and New Rivers into what is now southern West Virginia, Virginia, and

Table 3 Four Presbyteries at the Beginning

Year	Presbytery	West Virginia Territory
1781	Redstone	North Central and Northern Panhandle
1785	Abingdon	Southwest of Kanawha and New Rivers
1786	Lexington	Allegheny Mountains to Ohio River
1794	Winchester	Eastern Panhandle

Kentucky.[5] The following year, the synod created the Lexington Presbytery and set its boundaries as the Blue Ridge Mountains to the east and the Ohio River to the west, and between Redstone and Abingdon Presbyteries to the north and south. An outbreak of revival under the preaching of four itinerating probationers induced the founding of Winchester Presbytery in 1794.[6] Winchester was carved out of Lexington to eventually cover the "Northern Neck of Virginia," including much of West Virginia's Eastern Panhandle.[7] By the turn of the century every hill and holler of West Virginia was under the care of one these four presbyteries (Table 3).

In 1789, the restructuring efforts of the synods successfully created the first national Presbyterian denomination—the *Presbyterian Church in the United States of America* (PCUSA) Meanwhile, the work of evangelizing the main body of West Virginia fell to Lexington Presbytery, whose territory extended all the way to the Ohio River. As the work in this region grew to fifteen churches, Lexington Presbytery agreed that the Trans-Allegheny ministers could better coordinate their own work, since the mountains once again presented an obstacle, this time to convenient participation in Lexington's meetings. In 1838, the ministers of the fifteen Trans-

---

[5] *Winchester*, 59.

[6] *Lexington*, 75-77. This was an early manifestations of the Second Great Awakening on the Virginia frontier.

[7] The territory of Winchester contained some twenty-seven churches prior its founding (*Winchester*, 61-62). Only a few of these were in West Virginia.

Allegheny churches met at Lewisburg Presbyterian Church to convene the first stated meeting of the Greenbrier Presbytery. Their mission, as stated by Dr. John McElhenney, was to "set up the banners of Presbyterianism in the name of our God on these western waters." The Allegheny Mountains became the dividing line between the presbyteries, with the Greenbrier now taking full responsibility for all the territory that had once belonged to Lexington. In 1858, after coming to terms with its inability to evangelize the vast territory assigned to it, Greenbrier ceded Randolph, Barbour, Harrison, Upshur, Gilmer, and several other north-central counties back to Lexington Presbytery, comprising eight churches and more than two hundred members.[8]

In 1861, the *Presbyterian Church in the Confederate States of America* (PCCSA) seceded from the PCUSA, taking with it Greenbrier, Lexington, and Winchester presbyteries. From the time of the denomination's division, the lines of presbytery development obviously followed separate tracks. The Northern Panhandle's thirteen churches were already solidly in the hands of the Northern Church via their previous attachment to the Redstone Presbytery. The panhandle also contained an assortment of churches in the *United Presbyterian Church of North America* (UPCNA), formed in 1858 by the union of the *Associate Reformed Church* and the *Associate Reformed Presbyterian Church*. These historically Covenanter and Seceder churches would later expand the ranks of the PCUSA when their denominations united in 1958.

In 1863, the Northern Assembly created the Presbytery of West Virginia which immediately presumed to enroll Lexington's eight West Virginia churches. Both presbyteries stubbornly kept them on their rolls until the Presbytery of West Virginia acquiesced by an act

---

[8] *Lexington*, 110.

of conciliation in 1868. At that time, Lexington disenrolled six of the churches that had voluntarily adhered to the Northern Church, and the Presbytery of West Virginia disenrolled two that had not.[9] The PCUSA had attempted a similar tactic with the Presbytery of Winchester, by first transferring Winchester from the Old School Synod of Virginia into the New School Synod of Baltimore in the years leading up to the division. During the national division, it kept all Winchester's churches on its rolls by refusing to dismiss it from the Synod of Baltimore to the seceding Synod of Virginia. Winchester petitioned to be received into the Synod of Virginia anyway, which the Synod of Virginia "refused" on the grounds that a transfer had not been granted from Baltimore. However, in communicating this "refusal," the Synod hinted that if Winchester were to first join the PCCSA, it could be received without officially being dismissed from Baltimore. In this way, the Presbytery of Winchester joined both the PCCSA and the Synod of Virginia. Like Lexington's West Virginia churches, its ministers and churches remained dual-enrolled with both Assemblies until 1868.[10]

In 1889, the presbyteries of Lexington (PCUS) and West Virginia (PCUSA) finally agreed that the Parkersburg line of the Baltimore and Ohio Railroad would form a fixed boundary between them. This line did not affect the association of churches in other parts of the state that had already adhered to the Northern Assembly or would later choose to do so. Neither did it prevent Northern churches below the line from starting additional PCUSA churches, all of which remained in the Presbytery of West Virginia.

---

[9] The six were Buckhannon, French Creek, Bethel, West Fork, Glenville, and Clarksburg (*Lexington*, 415-16). The two were probably Mingo and Tygart's Valley.
[10] *Winchester*, 65-70. There were in fact two separate Winchester Presbyteries in the wake of the Old-School-New School Schism. Winchester (New School) first divided out in 1839 but reunited with the Winchester (Old School) in 1864 in solidarity with the Southern Church. *Winchester* (74-88).

In order to avoid confusion and better reflect its modest footprint in the state, the PCUSA's Presbytery of West Virginia renamed itself the Presbytery of Parkersburg in 1892, which "did not affect in any way the relationship of the churches that belonged to the Presbytery of West Virginia, nor did it limit in any way the boundaries of the presbytery."[11] By 1902, the presbytery aspired to form its own synod with a view to better addressing the unique needs of West Virginia. Requiring at least three presbyteries to bring this to pass, it divided to form Grafton Presbytery in north-central West Virginia, and then petitioned the Washington Presbytery to divide out the Northern Panhandle (formerly of Redstone) and create the Wheeling Presbytery in 1903. Once this was granted, the three (Wheeling, Parkersburg, and Grafton) united to create the Synod of West Virginia, PCUSA that same year.

After the dissolution of the Confederate States of America, the PCCSA had changed its name to the *Presbyterian Church in the United States* (PCUS). By 1888, the Greenbrier Presbytery comprised forty-five churches, twenty-one ministers, and 2,861 members.[12] Greenbrier remained the only PCUS presbytery wholly within the bounds of West Virginia until 1895, when the Kanawha Presbytery was divided out of the Greenbrier to cover the western portion of the state all the way up to Wood County. In 1912, the creation of the Tygart's Valley Presbytery allowed West Virginia to take back the north-central and eastern counties that Greenbrier had ceded to Lexington in 1858.

According to Lloyd McFarland Courtney, the Greenbrier historian, these three presbyteries—Greenbrier, Kanawha, and Tygart's Valley—"represented the work of the Southern Presbyterian Church in West Virginia."[13] With this tri-partition in place, the three presbyteries

---

[11] *Story of Presbyterianism*, 36.
[12] Price, *Historical Sketch of Greenbrier Presbytery*, 15.
[13] *Greenbrier*, 55.

immediately petitioned the Synod of Virginia and the Southern Assembly to create the Synod of West Virginia, PCUS. Courtney says that "one great thought" motivated their petition to create the synod: "It was erected for the purpose of meeting more effectively an opportunity in home missions which we believe is without parallel within the bounds of our church."[14] The Assembly granted their request, and the synod met for the first time at the Old Stone Church in Lewisburg in 1914. From this time until 1973, two separate Synods of West Virginia—Southern and Northern—co-existed within the state.

In 1928, the PCUS synod redrew its presbyterial lines to better accomplish their "one great thought." It dissolved Tygart's Valley and resorbed its territory into the Greenbrier and Kanawha presbyteries, significantly extending their domains into the northern and eastern parts of the state.[15] To compensate for the expansion, the synod created Bluestone Presbytery to focus more attention upon the southernmost counties. In this way, the synod was able to reclaim portions that had long been assigned to Abingdon Presbytery of the Synod of Appalachia, whose attention had consistently been elsewhere.[16]

Since the focus of this book is primarily the history of Presbyterianism in West Virginia prior to the rise of Modernism, the tracing of presbytery development could well end here. But in the interest of the completeness of this chapter at least, it should be noted that major changes occurred in both denominations in the twentieth

---

[14] *Greenbrier*, 57.

[15] It should be noted that all divisions, creations, and reorganizations required the cooperation and/or approval of presbyteries, synods, and general assemblies.

[16] *Greenbrier*, 36, 53; *Lexington* 145. A seldom mentioned "Guyandotte Presbytery" also existed for a few years (1968-1974) comprising portions of Bluestone and western Kanawha Presbyteries. Guyandotte, Kanawha, Bluestone, and Winchester were consolidated into Greenbrier and Shenandoah Presbyteries in 1974. Ellis, *Look unto the Rock*, 140.

century. In the Northern Church, the Auburn Affirmation of 1924 signaled that theological liberalism had won the Fundamentalist-Modernist battle waged since the turn of the century. In 1936, the *Orthodox Presbyterian Church* formed as a direct repudiation of the Northern Church's obviously liberal trajectory. Though the PCUS was more reticent to embrace theological liberalism, it eventually followed suit. As the mainline denominations became more theologically inclusive, scriptural authority and confessional subscription were no longer a point of contention. Modernism had effectively washed out the distinctions that formerly separated them, setting the stage for a reunion of the denominations.

In 1958, the aforementioned Covenanter and Seceder churches of the Northern Panhandle joined the Wheeling Presbytery when the UPCNA and the PCUSA united to form the *United Presbyterian Church in the United States of America* (UPCUSA). In 1973, the UPCUSA reorganized its synodical structures, merged the Synods of West Virginia and Pennsylvania, and turned the churches of the Wheeling Presbytery over to a newly-created Upper Ohio Valley Presbytery.

That same year, Southern Church ministers and churches who were frustrated by increasing theological liberalism withdrew from the PCUS to form the *Presbyterian Church in America* (PCA). This moved the historic Kanawha Salines Church and several other West Virginia churches from the PCUS into the PCA's New River Presbytery and the conservative, evangelical denomination that now styled itself as "the Continuing Church."[17] Then in 1974 the PCUS replaced the three presbyteries of its Synod of West Virginia with a

---

[17] For the story of the PCA's origins, see Sean Michael Lucas, *For a Continuing Church: The Roots of the Presbyterian Church in America* (Phillipsburg NJ: P&R Publishing Company, 2015). The first meeting of West Virginia's New River Presbytery occurred at Kanawha Salines in 1974.

single Greenbrier Presbytery, and the new Shenandoah Presbytery took over a large portion of the Eastern Panhandle. At this point, the PCUS Synod of West Virginia ceased to exist and the Synod of the Virginias took its place.[18]

Beside the rise of Modernism, the most significant change to mainline Presbyterianism in the twentieth century occurred in 1983. After one hundred twenty-two years, the Northern and Southern Churches finally put their long-standing differences behind them and reconciled. Their union created the largest presbyterian denomination in America, the *Presbyterian Church (USA),* or PC(USA). Four years later (1987), the PC(USA) created the West Virginia Presbytery, which, together with the Upper Ohio Valley and Shenandoah presbyteries, now covers the entirety of West Virginia. As of this writing, the West Virginia Presbytery contains almost 125 churches. The Shenandoah Presbytery has about thirty churches in the state, and the Upper Ohio Valley has around twenty. The PCA's New River Presbytery has ten.

Tracing the development of presbyteries may seem tedious to some readers, especially those unfamiliar with denominational bureaucracy. But this rehearsal should remind Presbyterians how essential these structures have been to Presbyterian identity and how vigorously Presbyterians have sought to maintain them even in the face of disruptive circumstances. Their goal has always been to build and maintain biblical connections that visibly represent the unity of the Body of Christ, enable pastors to effectively equip the saints, and support missions to destitute regions. Ministers and elders especially should be humbled to review how highly the Church has valued its sacred judicatories. The Rev. Dr. John McElhenney preached a similar reminder at the founding of Greenbrier Presbytery:

---

[18] The Synod of the Trinity, which replaced the Northern Church's Synod of Pennsylvania-West Virginia in 1983, provides some of these post 1970 details on its website, www.syntrinity.org.

Some seem to suppose that, as the business of the church can be done without them, it is only time and labor lost to attend her judicatories. Time in the general cannot be better spent. The interview which we have with one another; the sermons we hear preached; the interchange of sentiment and feelings in transacting the business of the church; and the united prayers which ascend to the throne of grace, all tend to enliven and animate the soul. And it not unfrequently occurs that the ministers and elders return home under a quickened influence, which is imparted to their respective congregations, and thus both pastor and people are benefited. This is not an imaginary representation, but a matter of practical understanding. If, then, we study our own interest, the interest of our people, and of the church at large; if we wish in the strength of our God to set up our banner, we must be punctual in attending the judicatories of the church.

5

MEMORIALS

PRESBYTERIANS HAVE A LONG history of memorializing recently deceased elders in presbytery minutes. For example, the Greenbrier Presbytery included the following statement in its memorial to John McElhenney in 1871:

> With this memorial we would record our gratitude to God for all that he accomplished through the life of his servant, and for the fruitful old age and happy death which closed his career in the church militant, to commence it anew in the church triumphant.[1]

But minutes are soon archived to gather dust, and names and accomplishments gradually disappear from popular memory. Historians later resurrect some of them for the generations to which they write. In that spirit, this history seeks to remind yet another generation of a few names and ministries that explain and exemplify the history of Presbyterianism in West Virginia.

The First Missionaries West of the Alleghenies

In 1838, McElhenney set in writing a few names of the first ministers west of the Alleghenies. Some of the earliest settlers still lived

---

[1] From the concluding paragraph of Greenbrier's memorial resolution following the passing of John McElhenney on January 2, 1871 (*Recollections,* 223).

when he first stepped into the Lewisburg pulpit in 1808. Colonel John Stuart, for instance, was fifty-nine at the time and served as an elder in the church for another fifteen years. No doubt he was one of McElhenney's sources in this statement:

> I have not been able to procure a single record or document which will throw even the least ray of light on the subject before me. It is not, then, to be presumed that I shall be able, with accuracy, to state the facts. All I can do is to state what I have collected from aged persons yet living, who, when young, were conversant with the first settlement of this country.

John McElhenney, then, is a primary source for what little is known of the first preachers on the western waters, though he saw fit to give only their surnames and a brief statement concerning the fruits of their labors:

> Soon after the settlement commenced, missionaries were sent into the country. The first so far as can be ascertained, was a Mr. Crawford, who, it is believed, came from the South Branch of the Potomac. The names of Frazer, Bead, and others, are mentioned, but of them we know nothing. There are persons now living who attribute their conversion to the instrumentality of those missionaries, and who, for more than sixty years, have proved faithful soldiers of the cross, and who have, indeed, been as burning and shining lights before the world.[2]

The Reverend John McCue (1753-1818)

A more reliable record of Presbyterianism in West Virginia begins in 1782, when Hanover Presbytery licensed and commissioned John McCue (b. May 8, 1753) to preach the gospel across the mountains.

---

[2] *Recollections*, 238. Courtney says his name was "Ben Edward Crawford" though he appears to be referencing this very quote (*Greenbrier*, 21). An "Edward Crawford" was briefly commissioned to Tygart's Valley in 1786 (*Greenbrier*, 37) and served as moderator in 1792 (*Lexington*, 417), placing him after John McCue. But McElhenney's Crawford was said to have come from the South Branch of the Potomac *prior* to John McCue.

Settling near the Greenbrier River, he organized the three Cornerstone Churches and distinguished himself as the first resident minister west of the Alleghenies.

McCue was a second-generation American whose parents migrated from Ireland in 1731. Like many pioneer ministers on the western waters, McCue graduated from Liberty Hall Academy near Lexington, Virginia.[3] As was the norm for ministerial aspirants, he tutored in theology for a while before being licensed and sent off as a missionary to Greenbrier County, where he preached to ready-and-waiting parishioners.[4] Upon his ordination at the Timber Ridge Church in 1783, McCue returned to start the Good Hope, Camp Union, and Spring Creek Churches. He then pastored at Good Hope (in Union) and Camp Union (in Lewisburg) and supplied the other for eight years, departing in 1791 to become the twenty-seven-year stated supply of the historic Tinkling Springs Church in Fishersville, Virginia. On the frontier, a dearth of ministers and remuneration precluded or delayed the luxury of pastoring a single congregation. So, as he did in Lewisburg, he also supplied the nearby pulpit of Staunton First Presbyterian for the first eight of his years at Tinkling Springs.

A contemporary account of a sacramental meeting in which McCue participated described him as "short, full set, of a ruddy countenance, pleasant and earnest in his services," but he was perhaps better known for being a controversialist with a fiery personality.[5] Henry Ruffner described an incident in which McCue had "suffered the irascibility of his constitution to get the mastery, for a moment,

---

[3] Liberty Hall Academy was later named Washington Academy, Washington College, and finally Washington and Lee University. The original Liberty Hall burned down in 1803, and its ruins, now listed on the National Register of Historic places, can still be visited on campus in Lexington.

[4] Montgomery, *History of the Old Stone Presbyterian Church*, 13. He read theology under James Waddell, pastor of Tinkling Spring.

[5] Quoted in Montgomery, *History of the Old Stone Presbyterian Church*, 14.

over his Christian equanimity." In a confrontation with an unnamed "gentleman," the man "used provoking language" but declined a fight because of McCue's "parson's coat." McCue is said have advanced upon him and responded, "Never mind the coat, sir. Never mind the coat."[6] His temperament was infamous enough to also earn several bitter mentions in the journals of John Smith, a Methodist circuit-rider, whom McCue repeatedly confronted with accusations of proselytizing. Apparently, alleged Smith, McCue had once threatened him with a stick.[7]

While at Tinkling Springs, it came to light that McCue was a member of a Masonic fraternity. Hints of this had first surfaced in Monroe County, when the Union Church discovered what appeared to be Masonic symbols on its foundation stones. At Tinkling Springs, the Lexington Presbytery inquired outright whether the rumors were true, to which McCue replied in the affirmative, though he was willing to withdraw his membership if requested. Nothing was done about it, however, and he retained both his ordination and his Masonic membership.[8]

McCue may have retained some of his sending presbytery's New Side sentiments. He once invited a Presbyterian revivalist into his Lewisburg pulpit who reportedly shocked the congregation by how much he sounded like a Methodist.[9] The Lexington Presbytery once chided McCue for his use of certain hymns in worship, particularly one "of very erroneous sentiments." McCue answered that he had been given the hymn after stepping into the pulpit and, in the spur of the moment, chose to "explicate" it rather than cause a scene. After he promised not to let it happen again, the presbytery let the matter rest.[10]

---

[6] Quoted in Montgomery, *History of the Old Stone Presbyterian Church*, 13-14.
[7] Banks, *200 Years*, 33.
[8] Banks, *200 Years*, 33.
[9] *Lexington*, 76.
[10] *Lexington*, 86.

One another occasion, the Presbytery asked him to explain himself after he voted against censuring a tavern-owner for permitting dancing on his premises. McCue replied that a vote implied the right to dissent and that impingement in this matter could lead to spiraling entanglements into "undue delay of marriage, idleness, gluttony, backbiting, slandering, wagering, and traveling on the Lord's Day."[11]

More seriously, in 1815 McCue was implicitly accused of beating one of his slaves repeatedly on the Lord's Day, interrupted only by his obligation to preach a sermon.[12] The abolitionist minister George Bourne had published incendiary accusations against the entire presbytery, saying "it was impossible to conceive the horrors of Slavery as practiced in Virginia even by Members of the Church and Ministers themselves."[13] After Bourne publicly refused to name names (he identified McCue's actions in a later, private communication), both the presbytery and the general assembly (on appeal) tried, convicted, and defrocked him for slander and other charges. At one point in the trial, Bourne confessed to "an irritable temper," "indecorous expressions," and "actions incompatible with the Charitable sensibilities which the Gospel enjoins."[14] The accusation against McCue was never adjudicated, though Banks says the trial "would indicate that [the accuser] was not known for his veracity."[15] Accounts imply that Bourne was known to make false accusations to further his abolitionist agenda.[16]

On Sunday, September 20, 1818, at the age of sixty-six, McCue died tragically while making his way to worship at the Tinkling Springs

---

[11] Quoted in Banks, *200 Years*, 34. See also Rice, *The Allegheny Frontier*, 303.
[12] *Lexington*, 90-93.
[13] Quoted in *Lexington*, 90.
[14] Quoted in *Lexington*, 92.
[15] Banks, *200 Years*, 34.
[16] Regardless of Bourne's ethics, the story illustrates strong anti-slavery sentiments among some early Presbyterians many decades prior to the Civil War.

Church. The following month, New York's *Commercial Advertiser* published this oddly descriptive death notice:

> Near Fredericksburg, Virg on Sunday the 27th ult. the Rev. John McCue; he was thrown from his horse, in his own lane, and killed dead on the spot! He was on his way to Tinkling Spring, alone, (his family having set out a little earlier than he did) riding a young horse not thoroughly tamed—he had not proceeded far when a small negro boy saw the horse running and plunging with great impetuosity—he presently saw his master fall—his head struck a stake, and the whole brain was dashed out! His own little daughter, the only one of the family who had remained at home, was the first white person who reached the fatal spot. What an awful spectacle! What an overwhelming scene! Though a child, she manifested a presence of mind, and a propriety of behavior, on the occasion, that would have reflected honor on mature years.[17]

The Reverend Benjamin Grigsby (1770-1810)

After McCue's departure in 1791, the Cornerstone Churches were without a minister until Benjamin Grigsby came to Lewisburg in 1794. Grigsby had also attended Liberty Hall Academy, graduating around 1789 and then reading theology under William Graham. By this time, Lexington Presbytery had divided out of Hanover to cover the territory between the Blue Ridge Mountains and the Ohio River. After a three-year probationary stint in Tidewater Virginia, Grigsby made his way to Greenbrier County in 1794. The churches had been without a pastor for three years by this time and were in decline. McElhenney later blamed this gap for the sorry state of religion when he came in 1808. Neither Grigsby's frequent absences during his tenure nor the eight empty years that followed his departure helped matters.[18] Though he stayed only six years, he must have made an impression—the name

---

[17] Vol. 21, Issue 60 (October 6, 1818), 2. Transcribed from a scan uploaded to John McCue's entry on Findagrave.com. The abbreviation "ult." means "ultimo," which in this context refers to the previous month. The date in the statement was wrong.
[18] Banks, *200 Years*, 56.

"Grigsby" was taken up into the community and passed on among several generations of Greenbrier children. The Lewisburg church's historian concluded that he had been "a popular and promising minister."[19]

In spite of popularity and promise, Grigsby left the church around 1800 or 1801 to return to a congregation in Norfolk where he had previously itinerated and where his ministry received more acclaim. Though many revivalists had travelled through Virginia during the Second Great Awakening, Grigsby was "the real reviver of Presbyterianism in Tidewater Virginia south of the Rappahanock."[20] Episcopalianism ruled the Tidewater, but "the inhabitants of Norfolk in Virginia, of Presbyterian persuasion" had sent a request for a minister in 1788. Both Grigsby and Archibald Alexander had been commissioned simultaneously in 1791 as Lexington's first candidates for ministry. Alexander had then traveled north to Cumberland and Grigsby to the Tidewater area. He preached frequently in Norfolk during his probation and was known to return from time to time even during his tenure in Lewisburg.[21] He was obviously fond of the place. It may be that one of these visits convinced him to leave Lewisburg for good.

Questions surround his departure from the Old Stone Church: Why, in 1798, did the congregation prepare an unprosecuted call to bring back John McCue in the middle of Grigsby's tenure?[22] Though he had left the church for Norfolk around 1801, why did Grigsby not petition presbytery to dissolve the pastoral relationship until three or four years later, in 1804? Why did he not request his credentials be transferred from Lexington to Hanover Presbytery, in whose

---

[19] Montgomery, *History of the Old Stone Presbyterian Church*, 30.
[20] *Winchester*, 5; See also *Lexington*, 75.
[21] Banks, *200 Years*, 36; *Lexington*, 75.
[22] Banks, *200 Years*, 28.

The Grigsby House is three miles east of Lewisburg on the Greenbrier River in Caldwell.

boundaries his new ministry lay? Why did he not appear when Lexington finally ordered him to give an account of himself in 1808? Why did he wait until 1809 to finally request a transfer to Hanover, eight years after leaving Lewisburg and only *after* John McCue had personally corresponded with him?[23] These irregularities were highly unusual in the well-ordered world of Presbyterianism, hinting that less-than-complementary details have not been passed down. They put the writer in mind (figuratively) of a man hiding a mistress, who, upon discovery, does all he can to avoid accountability. The minister may have been in the mountains, but apparently his heart was at the beach. On what might be a coincidental note, thirty-six-year-old Grigsby married seventeen-year-old Elizabeth McPherson in Norfolk in 1806.[24]

Grigsby died in 1810 at the young age of forty. His regal, imposing, obelisk-shaped memorial stands next to a paved courtyard-walkway, oddly enough in the Trinity Episcopal Cemetery in Portsmouth, Virginia. The inscription remembers him as "the first pastor of a Presbyterian church in Norfolk" and that he "fell a martyr to the yellow fever."

Whatever his achievements elsewhere, Grigsby's most notable contribution to Presbyterianism in West Virginia was simply the construction of the historic Old Stone Church in 1796. During his brief pastorate, the congregants moved from their log building on a country farm, a mile-and-a-half out of town, to the immediate outskirts of newly-named Lewisburg. There they built the historic structure and took the name Lewisburg Presbyterian Church. Both Grigsby and elder John Stuart, a stone-mason, had already built their own grand homes using Greenbrier County's native limestone. The rock would serve just as well for the construction of the new meeting house. Over 200 years later, all three still stand—the Grigsby and Stuart homes continue as private residences, and the Old Stone Church remains the oldest meeting house still in use west of the Alleghenies.

---

[23] Banks, *200 Years*, 37-38.
[24] Banks, *200 Years*, 37; Montgomery, *History of the Old Stone Presbyterian Church*, 30.

The Reverend John McElhenney, D.D. (1781-1871)

The Reverend Dr. John McElhenney was born in South Carolina on March 22, 1781. He came to the Old Stone Church pulpit in 1808, age twenty-seven, as an alien to the Commonwealth, the Shenandoah Valley, and the western waters.[25] Unlike his predecessor, McElhenney came to stay. And stay he did—for nearly 63 years, until his death on January 2, 1871, less than three months shy of his ninetieth birthday. Upon his passing, the church session memorialized him: "He was spared to preach to three generations in the same families, and to lay the hand of blessing on the head of the fourth."[26] His long and diligent tenure earned him the reputation as the greatest Presbyterian missionary and pastor to ever minister on the western waters.

The best source for information concerning McElhenney's ministry comes from his own hand—from the self-edited, published version of his Semi-Centenary Sermon delivered on the fiftieth anniversary of his arrival in Lewisburg.[27] In attendance at the celebration were many old friends and former students, including his future assistant, the Rev. John Calvin Barr, and the famed Dr. William S. Plumer of Pittsburgh's Western Theological Seminary. Several new ruling elders were ordained after the sermon, including the Hon. Samuel Price and "the lamented" Davis S. Creigh.[28] Stuart Robinson

---

[25] McElhenney was actually ordained in 1809. After being licensed and commissioned as missionaries, candidates would travel for one or more years to needy areas where eager-and-waiting congregants would issue a call. This call would then be taken back and prosecuted at a later presbytery meeting, often the following year. Thus, in some cases, starting years at particular churches might be licensure years. See Montgomery, *History*, 36-37; E. C. Scott, *Ministerial Directory of the Presbyterian Church, U.S.: 1861-1941* (Austin TX: Press of Von Boeckmann-Jones Co., 1942) 460.

[26] *Recollections*, 220.

[27] Reprinted as an appendix in *Recollections*, 245-263.

[28] Mr. Price later became a Lt. Governor of the Restored Government of Virginia and a U.S. Senator for West Virginia. Mr. Creigh has the unfortunate distinction of being the "West Virginia Martyr" because he was executed near the end of the Civil War for killing a Union soldier who was ransacking his house and threatening his

This portrait of John McElhenney hangs in the lobby of the Old Stone Church.

later wrote of the occasion, "Had such an event occurred in some of our large cities, how would all the journals of the land teem with grave editorial remarks and expressions of reverence in honor of the patriarch!"[29]

Like McCue and Grigsby before him, McElhenney attended Washington College and then read theology under the college president, who was at that time the Rev. Dr. George Baxter. McElhenney wrote that his original plan had been to attend Yale, his father's alma mater, but settled for Washington College after learning of an outbreak of yellow fever in New Haven.

---

family. He was later judged and hanged by a Union kangaroo court without being permitted to defend his actions. See Price, *Historical Sketch of the Greenbrier Presbytery,* 31-32. Price is buried in the Stuart family burial ground and Creigh in the Old Stone Church Cemetery.

[29] *Recollections,* 151-52.

In 1808, Lexington Presbytery commissioned him to the western waters, with a letter-in-hand commending him as "a young man of unblemished character, and we entertain strong hopes that he will be a respectable minister of the Gospel."[30] That spring, he itinerated for eight weeks, starting at Lewisburg and moving up through the "wilderness" of the Kanawha Valley to the Ohio River and then back, preaching all the way. Upon finishing his mission, he returned to Lexington where the presbytery had received a request from Lewisburg for him to serve as stated supply until a call could be prosecuted the following year. He was ordained in April of 1809 and installed as the pastor of Lewisburg Presbyterian Church that summer. His call specified that he was to alternate pulpits at Lewisburg and Union and to preach at least once per month at Spring Creek, during midweek services.

In addition to his ministerial duties, McElhenney worked as both a farmer and educator to supplement his "modest salary of six hundred dollars annually," which was "very often in arrears." His granddaughter recalled that "he was generally conceded to be the best farmer in Greenbrier County," and "his farm products always commanded a high price."[31] More significantly, shortly after his arrival he started the Lewisburg Academy, through whose doors dozens of influential ministers and esteemed citizens (both men and women) came and went over the decades.[32] Fry states, "Of those students destined to enter the ministry, I may mention—Dr. William S. Plumer, Rev. Henry Ruffner, D.D.; John H. Lin, a prominent Methodist minister; Rev. Jehu Shuck, a Baptist missionary; Rev. John Steele, of Monroe; Rev. James B. Slater, and others."[33] McElhenney remained

---

[30] Montgomery, *History of the Old Stone Presbyterian Church,* 36.

[31] *Recollections,* 61-62. To judge the modesty of $600 would require knowing what year Fry was referring to. Early in his career, $600 would have been extravagant.

[32] *Recollections* quotes a Zimmerman, who lists "legislators, great debaters, scientific men" (127).

[33] *Recollections,* 129. Also, the *160th Anniversary of Greenbrier County Commemorative Booklet* published in 1938 lists additional exemplary graduates: "Alex Reynolds, Brigadier General in the Confederate Army; Samuel Reynolds, a Colonel in the

president of the Academy until 1860, when the threat of war disrupted its operations.[34]

In his "Reminiscences of Dr. John McElhenney, D.D.," John Calvin Barr related a touching story concerning the teacher's reunion with one of his most famous pupils immediately following the Civil War. Though McElhenney had freed his own slaves years before the war, his heart (and that of most of Greenbrier County) had been with the South.[35] Dr. William S. Plumer, on the other hand, had been teaching at Western Seminary in Pittsburgh during the war. When it was over, Plumer had occasion to visit Lewisburg but was reticent to see McElhenney, fearing that the "feelings of his old friends had changed toward him." Dr. Barr encouraged him to visit McElhenney and offered to accompany him:

> As we entered the front gate at the lower end of the lawn in front of the Doctor's residence, he recognized from his door his dear old pupil, and came walking down the lawn, with his venerable head uncovered, and holding both arms wide open. Dr. Plumer, taking off his hat, walked on into his arms, and laid his head on his shoulder, and wept. The old teacher said, in his clear, strong voice, "William, how are you?" The younger could only sob out, "God bless you, Dr. McElhenney." Of all meetings we have ever witnessed between two venerable friends, that was the most touching and affecting.[36]

---

same army; Col. William Procter Smith, Chief of Engineers on General Lee's staff, who had large part in planning the fortifications of Richmond; and Alex F. Matthews, who had the distinction of winning the degree of A. M. from the University of Virginia in one year." Transcribed by Lori Samples from a booklet passed down to her from her grandfather, Accessed December 16, 2018, www.wvgenweb.org/greenbrier/history/160th10.html.
[34] *Inventory*, 254.
[35] This apparent contradiction will be explored in Chapter 7.
[36] *Recollections*, 166. The context for Plumer's anxiety and relief includes the national publication of what many in the Southern Church viewed to be his apparent capitulation to the demands of his church and presbytery to support the Federal government from his pulpit in Allegheny, Pennsylvania. The controversy was publicized in *The Christian Observer* in August of 1862. Cf. "Difficulty in Dr.

From his arrival in Lewisburg until 1819, McElhenney was almost alone in the work of the ministry. His own account gives the best picture of the magnitude of his responsibilities during this time:

> To understand what was necessary to maintain and promote the interests of Presbyterianism in this region fifty years ago, we must look at what was then the state of the country. When I settled here, and for many years after, there was no Presbyterian minister on the east nearer than Lexington, none on the west this side of the Ohio, and none north or south for at least one hundred miles. I was thus placed not far from the centre of a region of country at least two hundred miles square, in which there was no Presbyterian minister but myself; and whatever was to be done to promote the interests of our cause must be done by me, for there was none other to do it; and this rendered it necessary that my labors should not be confined to the congregations of which I was Pastor, as extensive as they were. Although there were eight points where I preached occasionally and administered the sacraments in the counties of Greenbrier and Munroe, exclusive of Lewisburg and Union, yet, as there was no Presbyterian minister in any of the adjacent counties, I was frequently solicited to visit them, which I did as often as practicable. And in addition to preaching and administering the ordinances, funerals were to be attended, the sick were to be visited, and marriages celebrated.[37]

By the time Greenbrier Presbytery was founded in 1838, fifteen churches had been planted within that same territory, pastored by ten ministers, and "containing in all, twelve to fifteen hundred members." Another twenty years later, at his semi-centenary, he looked back over fifty years of ministry:

> I have preached no less than seven thousand and eight hundred sermons; one thousand of which have been funeral sermons. I have administered baptism thirteen hundred times, including both adults and infants. I have

Plumer's Church." *The Continuing Story,* accessed March 5, 2019, continuing.wordpress.com.
[37] *Recollections*, 254.

married one thousand five hundred couples. As to the number of times I have administered the Lord's Supper, and the addresses and exhortations I have delivered, I can form no idea.[38]

McElhenney was gratified to have been "identified" with the organization of churches in Pocahontas, Bath (VA), Alleghany (VA), Montgomery, Fayette, Nicholas, and Kanawha Counties. He was especially gratified to have seen many periods of revival, four of which were his most memorable—1831, 1834, 1849, and 1857—during which nearly 270 souls were added to the church.

After recounting the history of the Presbytery and the fruits of his own ministry, McElhenney closed his Semi-Centenary sermon with a sobering appeal that bears review:

It becomes me to look back over the years of my ministry, and prepare to render the account of my stewardship at that bar from whose decision there is no appeal. Need I tell you that this is the most serious thing, on which the eye of every minister of the gospel should be fixed during the whole period of his ministry? But is it not peculiarly solemn in the closing days of the service so long as that which God has graciously granted me strength to perform? And mine is not the only account that is to be rendered at God's bar. There you too must stand, and answer for the manner in which you have heard and improved God's instructions, sent to you by me. With scarcely a single exception, the oldest of those to whom I minister now were the youth and the little children when my services here commenced. Through your whole life, and thus far in the life of those that are younger, I have preached to you the unsearchable riches of Christ. I have "showed you publicly, and from house to house, testifying to all repentance toward God, and faith toward our Lord Jesus Christ." The ministry must be to each one of you, my long-loved flock, "the savior of life and to life, or death unto death." Amongst all the relations existing on earth, there is not another the

---

[38] *Recollections*, 260-261.

John McElhenney and his wife Rebecca are buried in the front courtyard of the Old Stone Church.

account of which at God's bar will be more solemn, or attended with more important eternal consequences, then that of pastor and people. May God grant, in his rich grace, that we may be prepared to give up our accounts with joy; for, if they are not rendered with joy, it must be with eternal sorrow.

McElhenney would live to minister another thirteen years past the delivery of this admonition, supported in his most senescent years by his assistant, the Rev. Dr. John Calvin Barr, who wrote the following upon his passing:

> It is not strange that Dr. McElhenney was so universally beloved and esteemed. He was one of the best specimens of true manhood. He was noble-hearted, just, true, honest, pure, and generous towards men. He was humble, trustful, faithful, and devoted as a servant of God. Standing near the old church in Lewisburg is a beautiful marble monument erected to his memory by his devoted people. Yet the monument which most grandly perpetuates his memory is the

wonderful work of his own hands — the churches he built up, and the men whom he educated, whose influence will live forever.[39]

The Reverend Henry Ruffner, D.D. (1790-1861)

Presbyterians should remember Henry Ruffner as the founder of Presbyterianism in the Kanawha Valley, including three prominent churches that still exist today; for his vocation as professor and president at Washington College (now Washington and Lee University); and for his influential anti-slavery efforts in the years leading up to the Civil War.[40]

Dr. Ruffner was born in the Shenandoah Valley on January 16, 1790. In 1796, his grandfather Joseph Ruffner and father Colonel David Ruffner moved the family to the Kanawha Valley to build the area's first saltworks on a 502-acre tract by the Kanawha River.[41] Young Henry Ruffner preferred scholasticism to salt, so in 1809, at age nineteen, he moved to Lewisburg to study at John McElhenney's classical school. He was so well prepared by McElhenney that he was able to move on to Washington College to finish the complete curriculum in only a year and a half. As was the way for ministers in the frontier regions, he was tutored in theology by the president of the college (again, Baxter) for an additional year before being licensed to preach by Lexington Presbytery in 1815.

For the next four years, the young licentiate preached up and down the Kanawha Valley. *The Society of Christians Called Presbyterians* gathered to hear him preach in two locations: on his father's property near the saltworks in Malden—a place known as "Colonel

---

[39] *Recollections*, 166-167. His wife Rebecca Walkup survived him by five years and was buried beside him. He married Rebecca in Lexington the year before they came to Lewisburg. Their marriage lasted for sixty-three years. Montgomery, *History of the Old Stone Presbyterian Church*, 34.
[40] Scott, *Ministerial Directory*, 625.
[41] *Kanawha*, 59-60.

Ruffner's Meetinghouse"—and at the courthouse in Charleston six miles downriver and to the north. At the same time, he also taught at and apparently paid for some of the construction of the new Mercer Academy near the courthouse. The wealthy Ruffner family's influence was still on display, as young Henry's work was subsidized by and built on land donated by his father.

In the fall of 1818, the Presbytery ordained Ruffner in Lexington, and he immediately returned to start one of the oldest churches in the Presbyterian Church in America.[42] Under his authority, the *Society for Christians called Presbyterians* organized in 1819 to become the united "Presbyterian Church on Kanawha at Charleston and at Kanawha Salines." At first, the church met in one place or the other under a single session but eventually divided in 1841 to become the Kanawha Presbyterian Church (PCUSA) and the Kanawha Salines Presbyterian Church (PCUS, later PCA). Still a third church divided from the Kanawha Church in 1872—ironically named the First Presbyterian Church of Charleston (PCUS). The origin of these churches has been related above. To this day, all three claim to have been constituted in 1819 by the famed Henry Ruffner, and each claims the prestige of being the lineally original church.

Ruffner did not stay to pastor the church he founded. Soon after, he embarked on a career at his alma mater Washington College, progressing from Latin and Greek professor in 1819 to president in 1838. In 1847, Ruffner wrote a widely-distributed anti-slavery pamphlet called "Address to the People of West Virginia." The controversy of the pamphlet occasioned his retirement from the presidency in 1848, whereupon he returned to the Kanawha Valley around 1850.

With an eye toward finishing out his years in serenity, he bought

---

[42] "Fifty Oldest Churches in the PCA," PCA Historical Center, accessed March 27, 2019, www.pcahistory.org/churches/fiftyoldest.html.

property seven miles up Campbell's Creek and unsuccessfully tried his hand at sheep farming. Thankfully he was still a preacher, so he returned once again to the pulpit of the church he had started thirty years before. Stuart Robinson had left Kanawha Salines two years earlier, and Ruffner may have served as pulpit supply until they called their next pastor in 1853. When the pulpit became vacant once again in 1857, Ruffner again appears in the records as the moderator of the session and the church's stated supply.[43] When he died in 1861, he was buried in the small family plot a few hundred yards north of the church.[44] Toward the end of his life, he expressed regret that he had not stayed home all those years to minister in West Virginia. He wondered perhaps whether he could have accomplished more if he had spent his life preaching in the hills and hollers of the Kanawha Valley.[45] Henry Ruffner's son, William Henry Ruffner, wrote the following about his father's final years:

> During the decade preceding the Civil War, Dr. Ruffner foresaw the approaching catastrophe, as is shown by his Union speech delivered during that period, and it depressed him grievously in both body and mind, and no doubt shortened his life. About the time that the Cotton

---

[43] *Kanawha* 5-6

[44] Though the location is common knowledge to most locals, it is not publicized. I located it using descriptions, internet photos, and google maps on an out-of-the-way spot on an industrial property nearby. The company maintains the grounds of the cemetery, though the stones themselves are in poor condition.

[45] Specifically, he regretted that he did not stay to foster a short-lived church he had started in Teays Valley at the same time as the Kanawha Church. He also regretted that he was unauthorized to organize a church up the Pocatalico River when he was only a licentiate. Instead, he turned those congregants over to another preacher who successfully started a Methodist church. He did not begrudge this—he and the preacher were friends, and he felt that some religion was better than none at all. But he felt the loss for his denomination. He also regretted that, during his brief time preaching in the Kanawha Valley, he had focused too much on outreach to rural areas, and not enough on areas where churches were likely to be more viable in the long term. W. H. Ruffner, "The Ruffners. No. IV. Henry," *West Virginia Quarterly Historical Magazine*, April 1902, accessed March 13, 2019, transcribed at www.wvculture.org/history/antebellum/ruffnerhenry01.html.

The Ruffner Cemetery in Malden. The center stone is Henry Ruffner's.

States seceded his nervous system broke down utterly, and he was no longer able to preach. Gradually his strength failed without any attack of acute disease. His mind continued clear and that sweet peacefulness of spirit which had always characterized him never changed. His trust in God and his own hope in the future retained firm to the latest hour. He ceased to breathe December 17, 1861, aged 71 years and 11 months.[46]

The Reverend James Moore Brown, D. D. (1799-1862)

James Moore Brown was born on September 13, 1799 in Rockbridge County, Virginia, to Samuel and Mary Moore Brown. Descended from a Scots-Irish immigrant grandfather, Presbyterianism ran deep in James Moore Brown's blood. His father and four of his eight siblings were also Presbyterian ministers, and several of their children either became or married ministers (one spouse was R.L. Dabney).[47] Like many of his ecclesial "fathers and brothers" in West

---

[46] Ruffner, "The Ruffners. No. IV. Henry."
[47] *Kanawha*, 103.

Virginia, Brown attended Washington College in the early 1820s, foregoing his plan to attend Princeton—his father's alma mater—in order to care for his recently widowed mother and younger siblings. Following graduation, college president George Baxter tutored him for a year in theology and ministry.

Lexington Presbytery licensed Brown to preach on April 23, 1824, and sent him to Berkeley County (WV) to serve as stated supply for churches at Gerrardstown, Tuscarora, and Falling Waters. At the conclusion of this two-year probationary period, he married Mary Ann Bell of Winchester on September 26, 1826. Four days later (two of which were exams!), Winchester Presbytery ordained and installed him as pastor of the three Berkeley County churches. For nine years he took ministerial charge over a thirty-mile stretch of the Northern Neck of Virginia:

> Here he labored like an apostle, earnestly, faithfully, and successfully. On alternate Sunday mornings he preached at one or the other end of this field which, with an eight-mile ride on the horse back, permitted him to preach to the Tuscarora congregation each Sunday afternoon. During the week he explored the destitute regions round about and established preaching places. The Lord blessed his labors and many souls were added to the bride of Christ.[48]

In 1831, a revival in his congregations led to the reception of one-hundred twenty additional members. By the time he finished his ministry in Berkeley County, the Falling Waters church had increased from thirty-seven members to one hundred thirty-six, Gerrardstown had increased from ninety-three to one hundred fifty-nine, Tuscarora from sixteen to seventy-seven, and still another struggling church, Back Creek, from seven to fifty-seven. Winchester Presbytery minutes show that Brown had also been heavily involved in presbytery and

---

[48] *Kanawha*, 103-104. Scott, *Ministerial Directory*, 86.

assembly business—sitting on many committees and commissions, supplying at other churches, preaching installation services, and moderating presbytery meetings.

In 1834, he resigned his pastorate to serve as an assembly missionary in Prince Edward County, Virginia. In April 1837, Winchester dismissed him back to Lexington Presbytery, which installed him as the pastor of *The Presbyterian Church on Kanawha and at Kanawha Salines* on September 2nd of that same year.

The start of Brown's twenty-five-year tenure in the Kanawha Valley coincided with the founding of Greenbrier Presbytery. John McElhenney preached his installation service in 1837 and then presbytery's inaugural service in 1838. As he had for Winchester, Brown immediately dove into the new presbytery's business, serving as treasurer until his death in 1862, as Stated Clerk from 1849 to 1855, and as moderator at least three times.[49]

In 1840, his Kanawha Salines congregation built the beautiful permanent structure that still stands in Malden. In 1841, Brown oversaw the division of the two congregations into separate churches, presenting this resolution for the session's approval: "Resolved, that Greenbrier Presbytery be requested to divide the Kanawha Church by constituting a church to be known by the name of Kanawha Salines Church."[50]

Following the division, Brown took the Kanawha Church, and Stuart Robinson was called to lead the Kanawha Salines Church. Brown had helped raise Robinson during his time in the Northern Neck, had taught him at William Henry Foote's Academy in Romney, and had helped pay for his college tuition. No doubt it was a special privilege to

---

[49] *Greenbrier*, 116.
[50] Session Minutes, September 1st, 1841, *Kanawha Presbyterian Church* (photocopy). The Kanawha Salines Presbyterian Church in Malden, West Virginia, is now a congregation of the Presbyterian Church in America; *Kanawha*, 109.

see his "son in the faith" come into a pastorate so near to his own, and even more so to preach his installation sermon at Kanawha Salines.

During his busy ministry, Brown found time to write a book, published in 1854 as *The Captives of Abb's Valley: A Legend of Frontier Life.*[51] Brown tells the "melancholy legend of Abb's Valley," the true story of how, early one July morning in 1786, Shawnee Indians slaughtered his grandparents and all but three of their children and kidnapped his mother and uncle away to Canada. After she was ransomed from her captivity three years later, Mary Moore resettled elsewhere in the Valley of Virginia and married the Rev. Samuel Brown, never to return to or speak of Abb's Valley again. From this union came a plethora of Presbyterians and ministers who passed on their faith for generations to come. The small, captivating book fully displays Moore's gifts as a story-teller, his ministerial concern for the reader, and his devotion to his mother and family. Rev. Brown was named for the murdered grandfather of that story—James Moore.

The Rev. Dr. Brown passed away from typhoid fever in 1862 along with two of his six children. The spring presbytery meeting was to be held in Muddy Creek that year, close to Lewisburg nearly one-hundred arduous miles on horseback from Kanawha County. As was his custom, he had probably prearranged to preach once or twice a day along the way. Upon nearing Lewisburg, his first stop was Frankford, some twenty miles north of his destination, to visit the home of his adult son, John Calvin Brown. His twenty-two year old daughter, Mary Roberta Lavina, and another son, twenty-seven year old James Morrison, had been visiting there for some time.

Upon his arrival, he found Mary sick with typhoid fever, and she passed away on April 26th. James Morrison soon fell ill as well and

---

[51] (Philadelphia: Presbyterian Board of Publication and Sabbath-School Work, 1854).

The Frankford Cemetery a few miles north of Lewisburg. James Moore Brown's stone is center. The death year on his marker is mistakenly etched as 1867. His daughter Mary rests at his right and his son James to his left. The resting site of his oldest son, John Calvin Brown, 25 year pastor of the Kanawha Salines Church, is marked by the large stone to the left.

died twenty days later. Then, finally, Dr. Brown himself succumbed to the same fever on June 7th in the Lewisburg home of his dear friend, John Calvin Barr. He was buried near his children in the Frankford Cemetery of Greenbrier County.[52]

On April 28th, two days after his daughter's passing, he had recorded the following in his diary:

> What it is to issue in, God only knows. I feel that my family is in his hands and all safe there. I gave my children back to him as soon as he gave them to me. He has regenerated them by his Spirit, and thus to their father in a double sense. His disposal is kind and wise, I doubt not."[53]

---

[52] *Kanawha*, 115. Brown had previously lost two other children.
[53] *Kanawha*, 8.

The Reverend Stuart Robinson, D. D. (1814-1881)

Stuart Robinson was one of only three West Virginia ministers who had a "national reputation," the others being Henry Ruffner and William Henry Foote. Robinson's fame came to him after he left West Virginia for the border state of Kentucky, "where he rendered such notable service throughout the Synod of Kentucky and to the whole church, as pastor, seminary professor, editor, theologian, and author."[54] Before, during, and after the Civil war, his periodical publications became an influential Old School mouthpiece for the doctrine of the Spirituality of the Church

Robinson was born in Ireland on November 15, 1814. Before he was two, his parents immigrated to United States, where they settled first in New York and then finally in Berkeley County. At some point before or during his journey from Ireland, Robinson fell from his nurse's arms and sustained a life-long injury to his right arm and hand, providentially preventing him from becoming a farmer like his father.[55] After his mother died around 1826, his father entrusted him to the care of a German family in Martinsburg, who in turn made him the ward of the Rev. James Moore Brown. While under Brown's care and direction, Robinson attended William Henry Foote's Romney Academy and matriculated at Amherst College, Union Theological Seminary, and Princeton Theological Seminary.[56] Brown's guidance and material support culminated in Robinson's ordination as the pastor of the Kanawha Salines Church on October 8, 1842.

Robinson's pastorate at Kanawha Salines lasted only five years, but his time there was memorable and fruitful. The historian of the

---

[54] *Kanawha*, 5. Scott, *Ministerial Directory*, 616.

[55] Preston D. Graham, Jr, *A Kingdom Not of This World: Stuart Robinson's Struggle to Distinguish the Sacred from the Secular during the Civil War* (Macon GA: Mercer University Press, 2002), 13.

[56] *Winchester*, 494. He was awarded his Doctor of Divinity by Centre College in Danville KY in 1853.

Kanawha Salines church credits an unknown author with the following description of his ministry:

> He taught, and preached, and traveled up and down the valleys and over the hills and mountains of his new home. He was diligent in business, fervent in spirit, serving the Lord. He accomplished a mighty work in all that Kanawha country, preaching everywhere, organizing prayer meetings and Sunday schools in out of the way neighborhoods, and attaching the people to him as they had never been attached to any other minister. He read, studied, and wrote as he could catch the time, in his own little family room, in the presence of his wife and little children. He was full of missionary zeal; a live man; and wonderful worker, with the blessing of God always resting upon him.[57]

Robinson's life after West Virginia was busy and even more fruitful. He pastored in Frankfort, Kentucky (1847-52), supplied the Fayette Street Church (ARP) in Baltimore (1852-53), organized and pastored the Central Church of Baltimore (1853-56), co-organized the Synod of Baltimore (1854) taught at Danville Theological Seminary (1856-58), pastored the Second Presbyterian Church of Louisville (1858-81), and moderated the Southern General Assembly in 1869.[58] From 1862 until 1866, Robinson fled to Canada to escape persecution for taking an apolitical position on the war in his weekly periodical, the *True Presbyterian*. His reasons for this position will be explored later.

Robinson's national reputation came to him mostly through his publications. His periodicals were mouthpieces for the doctrine of the Spirituality of the Church before, during, and after the Civil War: The *Presbyterial Critic and Monthly Review* (1855-56), the *True Presbyterian* (1862-1865), and the *Free Christian Commonwealth* (1865-68).[59] While a professor at Danville Seminary (1858) he published his book *The Church of God as an*

---

[57] Quoted in *Kanawha*, 5. Robinson served as stated supply in 1842 and was installed as pastor in 1843.
[58] *Winchester*, 494.
[59] Graham, *Kingdom*, 279.

Essential Element of the Gospel. During his Canadian exile (1865) he published *Slavery as Recognized in the Mosaic Civil Law, Recognized Also, and Allowed, in the Abrahamic, Mosaic, and Christian Church: Being One of a Series of Sabbath Evening Discourses on the Laws of Moses.* He also published his *Discourses of Redemption as Revealed in Sundry Times and Diverse Manners* in 1866, a topic for which he held a special passion.

Upon his return from Canada in 1866, Robinson once again pastored the Second Presbyterian Church, where his "humanitarian and ministerial efforts would continue" until his death 1881. He and his wife started a "Negro orphans home" as well as Sunday schools for both African Americans and whites in their own home and throughout the city. One of these eventually grew large enough to become the Stuart Robinson Memorial Church. Robinson is interred in Louisville's Cave Hill Cemetery.[60]

The Reverend John Calvin Barr, D. D. (1824-1911)

Dr. John Calvin Barr should be remembered for his lengthy pastorate and for his conviction that a church is not truly Presbyterian unless it is connected to the larger church. He was born November 11, 1824, in Washington County, Pennsylvania, and married Maria B. Smith in 1859, making him kin by marriage to James Moore Brown. He graduated from Western Theological Seminary in 1858 and was ordained by the Ohio Presbytery that same year.[61] Dr. Barr's first ministry in West Virginia was as an assistant to the aging John McElhenney at the Lewisburg Presbyterian Church beginning in 1859. It was during this time that his brother-in-law James Moore Brown passed away at his residence in 1862. He served alongside McElhenney for 10 years, where a strong and familial bond developed between the two.

[60] Graham, *Kingdom*, 186.
[61] *Historical and Biographical Catalog of the Officers and Students of the Western Theological Seminary of the Presbyterian Church at Allegheny City, Penn'a, 1827-1885* (Allegheny PA: Published by the Seminary, 1885), 71. Scott, *Ministerial Directory*, 38.

In 1868 his family connections led him to Charleston, where he taught at the Charleston Institute, and to the Presbyterian Church on Kanawha, which later birthed the First Presbyterian Church.[62] He first served there as an assistant to the Rev. W. N. Geddes. But in 1872, when Geddes resigned for health reasons and Barr was up for the job, Barr made clear he wanted the church to return to its Presbyterian commitments, which meant that it must choose either the Presbyterian Church in the United States of America or the Presbyterian Church in the United States.

For the previous eleven years—since the start of the Civil War—the Kanawha Church had declined to send representatives to either denomination's presbytery or general assembly.[63] Like a microcosm of West Virginia itself, the church comprised supporters from both sides. But the State had seceded from Virginia nine years earlier, and the war was long over. That the church remained in its mottled, uncommitted condition is testimony to residual sentiments that still simmered beneath the surface long after the war (whether these were more concerned with slavery or ecclesiology will be discussed later). Though the lack of commitment to one or the other denomination created the pretense of unity within the congregation,

---

[62] *Kanawha*, 117.

[63] Ruth Putney Coghill, *The Church of 150 Years* (Charleston WV: First Presbyterian Church, 1969), n.p. See also Ruth P. Coghill, *The First Presbyterian Church Charleston West Virginia: A Brief History* (n.p., n.d.). Another less recent account (~1950) speculates that Barr kept out of the matter and that the determination to vote boiled up from within the congregation, which may have recently had an influx of new members from the Malden church (*Kanawha*, 120-121). This may be based on an even older account which says that "one hundred members of the old congregation, petitioned the Session that Presbyterial relations be resumed." Katie Bell Abney, *History of the Presbyterian Congregation and the Other Early Churches of "Kenhawha" 1804-1900* (Charleston, WV: First Presbyterian Church, 1930), 32. Both might be true—that Barr encouraged adherence to an Assembly, and the congregation petitioned the session in response. The answer may lie in the records of the Kanawha Church held by the Presbyterian Historical Society in Philadelphia, which I have not yet had opportunity to explore.

the church was for all intents and purposes "very nearly in the position of a congregational church" and was thus disjoined from the larger Church.[64]

In order to have their pastor, the church complied with Barr's wish, and the twenty-three people who voted to go with the PCUSA kept the church's name, the manse, and the larger portion of the property. The other 153 took the sanctuary, a smaller portion of the lot, and became the First Presbyterian Church of Charleston (PCUS). By all accounts, the division of church and property was agreeable and orderly, if melancholy.[65] The church had kept itself in limbo for over a decade in order to avoid just such a split. Ultimately, Barr acted upon the biblical truth that the church's independence was not unity at all.[66] But for all his theological correctness on that point, there is no public record that he ever addressed the specific issues that had sparked the war, either before or after the vote.[67] When all was said and done, he himself went with the Southern church and continued as their pastor for thirty-six more years.

Dr. Barr died on September 8, 1911, and was buried in Spring Hill Cemetery, overlooking the city in which he ministered for so long. Both the First and Kanawha Presbyterian Churches have continued through to the present as prominent congregations in Charleston. Their meeting houses have always been a short walk from each other, and now they both coexist in the same denomination.

---

[64] *Kanawha*, 118.

[65] *Kanawha*, 118-122.

[66] Cf. Dennis E. Bills, *A Church You Can See*, 82: "Because particular churches are the building blocks of the visible church, the best opportunity for particular churches to pursue unity within the visible body of Christ is through denominational affiliation."

[67] *Kanawha*, 121.

Mr. John C. Bowyer (1815-1888)

For over thirty years, John C. Bowyer was janitor and sexton of the Old Stone Church, first as a slave, then as an employee.[68] He seems to have been mostly forgotten, though McElhenney's granddaughter Rose Fry (1847-1902) and Colonel John Stuart's great-granddaughter Margaret Lynn Price (1842-1917) provide a few personal references to him.[69] Both called him "uncle," a paternalistic term of endearment by which he was known in the community.[70] It is possible that a quote attributed in 1938 to "an aged sexton of the old church many years ago" was John Bowyer's. Concerning the longevity of the Old Stone Church building, the sexton is reputed to have said, "Jest keep it kivered and it'll last 'til judgement day."[71] If this sexton was Mr. Bowyer, the recollection of his colloquially expressed sentiments was apparently valued more than his name.

According to Fry, Dr. McElhenney first leased John Bowyer as a slave from an unnamed woman and put him to work at the church.[72] McElhenney had once owned slaves himself, but sometime before the war had freed and hired them to work his farm at a "fair wage."[73] Similarly, after Bowyer's emancipation, McElhenney himself paid a third of Bowyer's full salary in order to keep him on part-time at the

---

[68] Margaret Lynn Price, "Colonel John Stuart of Greenbrier" *The West Virginia Historical Magazine Quarterly* 5, no. 2 (1905): 124. Also, "John Boyer [*sic*]," *The Journal of the Greenbrier Historical Society* 7, no. 5 (2003): 93.

[69] Price, "Colonel John Stuart of Greenbrier," 119-127. Bowyer is not named in the official *History of the Old Stone Presbyterian Church*, even on the fifteen-name list of "Our Negro Members" found on p. 340.

[70] *Recollections*, 189; Price, "Colonel John Stuart of Greenbrier," 124.

[71] *160th Anniversary of Greenbrier County Commemorative Booklet*, 1938.

[72] According to historian Morgan Bunn of the community organization *Friends of the Old Stone Cemetery*, Bowyer's original owner, Luke Bowyer, died in 1819 and might have been his father. Bowyer was eventually transferred to his sister who died in 1853 (Email, March 18, 2019). Who owned him next is unknown, but he began working for the church in 1854.

[73] "He had freed his own Negro man" (*Recollections*, 170), and "His old slaves continued to work for 'Marse John' at fair wages" (189).

church. Fry says he was her grandfather's "right hand man," and that "a better sexton, or more reliable work-hand than this yellow man never lived; and grandfather would have considered himself ruined without John Bowyer!"[74]

As the church sexton, Bowyer cleaned the building, opened it for services, lit the fires, rang the bell, kept the grounds, and buried the dead. A search of the cemetery for stones dated between 1854 and 1888 would likely reveal hundreds of graves dug by his own hands, but he himself was not buried among them. He died on March 19, 1888, at age seventy-three and was laid to rest in the cemetery across the street from the white graveyard.[75] Fry says, "A simple stone marks his grave in the colored plot, and there were many who thought it would not have been inappropriate to lay him alongside of his white brethren, amidst the dust of hundreds whom he had committed to their last resting-place."[76] His funeral at the Old stone Church was reportedly well attended by blacks and whites alike, and the community took up funds to pay for the stone that now marks his grave.[77]

---

[74] *Recollections*, 189. Fry says that "Uncle John" was "more warmly attached to the whites than to his own race." "Yellow" was a term used during Fry's era (late 19th century) to describe light-skinned African Americans who were more socially accepted among whites. See Taunya Lovell Banks, "Colorism: A Darker Shade of Pale," *UCLA Law Review* 47 (2000), accessed June 6, 2018, digitalcommons.law.umaryland.edu/fac_pubs/217.

[75] Bowyer is listed in the 1880 US Census as a widowed mulatto male, 62 years of age; occupation: farmer; father's birthplace: "bastard." According to Bowyer's publically edited Find-A-Grave entry, he was married to Elizabeth Folden Bowyer. (Accessed June 6, 2018). He is listed twice in Greenbrier County records with different death dates—March 17 and 19; the latter is correct. The first entry lists a cause of death as Acute Diarrhea and the second as General Debility. In the first he is designated MBS (Male, Black, Single) and in the second as MB (Male, Black). Larry G. Shuck, comp., *Greenbrier County Death Records 1853-1901* (Athens, GA: Iberian Publishing, 1993), 25.

[76] *Recollections*, 190.

[77] Morgan Bunn, email, March 18, 2019. Ms. Bunn, a historian and cemetery restorer, has led the charge to repair his stone. She says, "The stone is being eaten away from the inside out by the support rebar rusting and stress created by the expanding of the rebar. The stone will be taken off the base, the rebar drilled out,

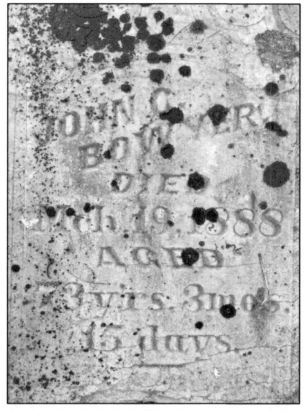

John Bowyer's resting place in the "Colored Cemetery" across from the Old Stone Church. The local cemetery preservation society is seeking to restore his gravestone.

John C. Bowyer's name deserves to be resurrected in minds of the church and community. Though his work was menial and mundane, the community apparently respected him for his faithfulness, longevity, and attention to detail. He served the Church, at first by compulsion and then of his own free will. The record does not tell us what other opportunities were available to him following his emancipation—

---

nylon and stainless rods put back into the stone, along with historic mortar to give the stone new internal strength and the cracks and missing stone replaced with historic mortar. The stone will then be given a new underground drainage system and base and should stand for another 200 years with few issues. There is little that can be done about the black spots (a combination of tree sap and pollution) though I shall try to remove some."

perhaps there were none. But he "always swore by what Mr. McElhenney said and did, both in the pulpit and out of it. He took his old master's every word and command as gospel truth, and carried out his instructions to the letter."[78] Thus it seems he stayed on willingly, out of affection for his pastor and the church. In spite of his three decades of faithful service and the respect it supposedly earned him, he was laid to rest in the "colored" cemetery and eventually forgotten, to the shame of the Church both then and today.[79]

Many other names could have been be included in this chapter, notable for their ministerial accomplishments: John Chavis, "a full-blooded Negro veteran of the Revolutionary War" who itinerated as a licentiate among both blacks and whites in southern West Virginia.[80]

---

[78] *Recollections*, 189.

[79] This lack of remembrance is being addressed according to Morgan Bunn. The Greenbrier Historical Society and the Friends of the Old Stone Cemetery are working on a community theatrical production that spotlights the life of John Bowyer based on Bunn's research.

[80] *Lexington*, 80-81.

Calvin Chaddock, Congregationalist and first pastor of the Kanawha Church; his successor Nathaniel Calhoun, a minister and medical doctor who left the church under mysterious circumstances;[81] Aretas Loomis, who introduced Presbyterianism to Tygart's Valley;[82] Asa Brooks, who was buried under the pulpit of the Clarksburg Church "so that the church would never be without a pastor"; Joseph Brown, brother to James Moore Brown and son of Mary Moore Brown, the "Captive of Abb's Valley"; John Calvin Brown, son of James Moore Brown and his twenty-five-year successor at the Kanawha Salines Church;[83] William T. Price, Pocahontas County minister who journaled his experiences as a Confederate Chaplain;[84] Loyal Young, Upshur County minister whose overture to the PCUSA assembly after the start of the Civil War split the church in West Virginia into North and South.[85] James H. Leps, "the distinguished and highly popular chaplain of the famous 31st Va. Regiment";[86] Matthew Lyle Lacy, an educator and respected successor to McElhenney at the Old Stone Church;[87] William Henry Foote, principal of the Romney Academy and historian of Virginia, North Carolina, and the Huguenots;[88] and William S. Plumer, famed author, theologian, and professor at Western Theological Seminary, whom Colonel David Ruffner first discovered at the Kanawha docks when he was merely a "steersman on his father's store boat."[89] Ruffner sponsored Plumer's education from McElhenney's Academy all the way through Washington College. All these and many more settled in, passed through, or went out from the hills and hollows of West Virginia. Many of them still rest there today.

---

[81] *Kanawha*, 95-99.

[82] *Greenbrier*, 26, 38.

[83] *Ministerial Directory*, 87

[84] *Ministerial Directory, 587*. Ellis, *Look unto the Rock*, 101-107.

[85] *Story of Presbyterianism*, 29.

[86] Price, *Historical Sketch of Greenbrier Presbytery*, 47. *Ministerial Directory*, 401.

[87] *Ministerial Directory*, 386.

[88] *Winchester*, 462. *Ministerial Directory*, 225.

[89] *Kanawha*, 71. *Ministerial Directory, 576.*

6

CONTROVERSIES, SCHISMS, AND DIVISIONS

IN THE EIGHTEENTH AND nineteenth centuries, three schisms altered the path of Presbyterianism across the nation. These were the Old Side-New Side Controversy of 1741, the Old School-New School Schism of 1837, and the split of the denomination into the Northern and Southern Churches in 1861. A brief review of each will show how these interrelated to impact Presbyterianism in West Virginia.

The Old Side-New Side Controversy

One effect of the Old Side-New Side Schism (1741-58) was to entrench revivalist pietism into Presbyterian religious culture in America. This pietism would later have a profound impact on the development of Appalachian mountain religion, which is discussed in the final chapter. Born of the Great Awakening's revivals and the preaching of George Whitefield, American pietism emphasized that ministers' personal religious experience was as important as (and maybe more important than) their confessional subscription, Bible knowledge, and education. Pietism broadened the Presbyterian church by encouraging the founding of alternative educational institutions that perpetuated pietism and by widening, if only slightly, the path of ordination for ministers. Most of the colleges and seminaries that educated later frontier ministers were founded in this freer educational climate. They perpetuated regional theological and methodological differences that would become important by and by.

The Old School-New School Schism

In 1801, the General Assembly of the Presbyterian church unilaterally approved a Plan of Union with the Congregationalist General Association to strengthen the ranks of ministers in the rapidly expanding church. The Plan of Union permitted Congregationalist ministers to participate in the church's courts, creating an influx of non-Presbyterian ministers who were not subject to subscription requirements and over whom presbyteries had little jurisdiction. Though the plan was intended to unify the church, ensuing tension laid the foundation for the division of the denomination.[1]

Congregationalism brought with it several theological aberrations from New England, where Calvinistic views on depravity, free will, and the atonement had been devolving since the days of Jonathon Edwards. Armed with a theology that gave them great confidence in the ability of the Presbyterian church to reform secular morality, a "New School" of Presbyterianism embarked upon a form of social engineering, albeit according to Christian principles. They relied heavily upon revivalist techniques, political engagement, and voluntary societies outside the church to accomplish their dream of a better, more Christian society.[2] On the other hand, the Old School affirmed confessional views on depravity and a sharp distinction between the domains of the secular and the sacred—that the business of the church was exclusively spiritual, and that it should be accomplished only through agencies of the church. The New School, then, could be

---

[1] *Lexington*, 101-103.
[2] Bradley Longfield, *Presbyterians and American Culture: A History* (Louisville KY: Westminster John Knox Press, 2013), 91-92. In this and the following section, I am indebted to both Longfield's book and Mark Noll's *The Civil War as a Theological Crisis* (Chapel Hill, NC: The University of North Carolina Press, 2006) for my understanding of relevant historical and theological contexts.

characterized by its emphasis upon renewing or reforming social structures, a consequence of an inadequate view of depravity. The Old School, with its concern for the preservation of doctrine and individual pietism, remained more focused on the transformation of the soul. This characterization may be reductive, but for simplicity's sake it explains the polarity that motivated the sides to act unilaterally against each other.

During the early nineteenth century, tensions over theology and polity continued to increase. Finally, in 1837, the General Assembly's Old School repealed the Plan of Union and declared several New School synods and presbyteries to be unconstitutional. At the following year's Assembly, the Old School majority refused to seat commissioners from the excluded presbyteries, and the New School responded by holding its own Assembly. For the next few decades, the church continued in disarray as competing assemblies and synods garnered the allegiances of churches across and within presbyteries throughout the Presbyterian church in America.

In the various histories of West Virginia's presbyteries, almost no mention is made of the direct effects of the Old School-New School Schism, even though presbyteries around the country were being claimed, created, or restructured to fit the new divisions of 1837 and 1838. It is possibly no coincidence that Greenbrier Presbytery, with its decidedly Old-School adherents, was formed at the start of the schism. Gill Wilson, the only historian to attempt a statewide overview of the activities of the Northern Church in West Virginia, wrote that churches were exploring the possibility of their own presbytery as far back as 1834. The minutes of the Presbyterian Church of Clarksburg confirm Wilson's observation:

> Information being received that the ministerial brethren of Lewisburg, Charleston, Parkersburg, Beverly, Middletown, and Morgantown are desirous that a Presbytery be organized embracing the Western Section

of Virginia therefore on motion Resolved that we do concur in the measure it being as we conceive preeminently calculated to promote the interests of the Redeemer's Kingdom in this destitute Region. Resolved that the Presbytery of Redstone and the Synod of Pittsburgh be petitioned at their ensuing meetings to take such measures as shall be necessary to carry the above object into effect.[3]

Wilson gives no further information, except to say that nothing came of it.[4] However, the mere timing of the "information being received" suggests it had something to do with climaxing tensions between the Old and New Schools.

Just four years later though, in September of 1838, the Clarksburg session appears to have had a change of mind: "Ordered that this Session represent to [Redstone] Presbytery their dissatisfaction of any attention in the limits of this Presbytery by which Harrison County would be thrown into another Presbytery."[5] At least two events had occurred in the interim: Their minister Asa Brooks had died, and the denomination had just recently divided into separate assemblies. It may be that the Greenbrier Presbytery was the eventual result of the explorations that had begun in 1834. It seems in the case of Clarksburg at least that it chose not to participate, expressing hints of ecclesiastical prejudice.

The Northern Church-Southern Church Split

The Christian abolitionist movement and the growing animosity between the Northern and Southern States brought the ecclesiastical crisis to a head. As hostility over slavery increased, and as abolitionism spread from New England throughout the Northern church, the stage was set for an official division of both the nation and the

---

[3] Session Minutes, October 1, 1834, Clarksburg Presbyterian Church, Clarksburg WV.
[4] *Story of Presbyterianism*, 30.
[5] Session Minutes, September 15, 1838.

denomination. With weakening ties to the monolith of confessional theology and the pervasive influence of the Enlightenment, the religious commitments of the entire nation became extremely susceptible to the influences of their immediate cultural contexts (i.e., North and South). Within the existing denominational mechanisms, these regional commitments paved the way for the splitting of the Church, each side claiming its own manifest destiny, willing to permit or support taking up literal and figurative arms against the other. This also set the stage for the further development of a unique ecclesiology, born of Old School opposition to Congregationalist idiosyncrasies and born again of Northern pressures upon the Southern Church. The development of this ecclesiology—the doctrine of the Spirituality of the Church—would permit the Southern church to take the side of the Confederacy, irrespective of personal convictions concerning slavery itself.

Secular and religious pressure upon the southern Presbyterians catalyzed the actual split of the church. Oaths were not uncommon in civil society, and ministers did not object to them as a civil duty, but when state agents required them of ministers as representatives of the church, they strongly objected, even to the point of risking ministries and livelihoods. Likewise, the Gardener Spring Resolutions of the 1861 General Assembly drove a deeper wedge between the Northern and Southern church. The resolutions obligated ministers "to promote and perpetuate, so far as in us lies, the integrity of these United States, and to strengthen, uphold, and encourage the Federal Government in the exercise of all its functions under our noble Constitution; and to this Constitution in all its provisions, requirements, and principles, we profess our unabated loyalty." In response, Charles Hodge and other Old Schoolers protested that "we deny the right of the General Assembly to decide the political question, to what government the allegiance of

Presbyterians as citizens is due, and its rights to make that decision a condition of membership in our Church."[6]

But the damage was done. Not only were the southern states now pitted against the North, the Northern Church had made itself the enemy of the Southern Church. The stage was again set for the Southern Church to declare itself a separate denomination, free from both Federal coercion and the New School's secular agenda. This happened later that same year (1861), as the nation itself was rending, when the Southern Presbyterians held a General Assembly to declare themselves the *Presbyterian Church of the Confederate States of America*. After the Confederacy ceased, they changed their name to the *Presbyterian Church in the United States* (PCUS), by which they were called until the denominations reunited in 1983.

In this way Old School theology became married to the Doctrine of the Spirituality of the Church and eventually settled overwhelmingly in the South.[7] Regionally, the social and theological influences of Congregationalism and the New School decreased as distance from its New England fountainhead increased. The Spirituality Doctrine inhered in Southern Church where abolitionism was almost universally perceived as an extremist secular agenda forced upon the Church's conscience. And since the Church now had a plethora of Old School training institutions divorced from New England influences (as a result of the Old Side/New Side changes from the previous century), the marriage between the Old School Southern Church and the Spirituality Doctrine persisted for decades to come.

---

[6] Transcribed with supporting documentation at "The Gardiner Spring Resolutions," *PCA Historical Center*, Accessed March 21, 2019, www.pcahistory.org.
[7] Many Old School proponents existed in the Northern Church and New School within the Southern Church, though the overwhelming concentrations of New School in the North and Old School in the South merit the generalization.

West Virginia Presbyterianism and the National Question

Questions naturally arise concerning the impact of these divisions on West Virginia Presbyterians, particularly whether the adherence of most to the Southern Church meant they implicitly supported the institution of slavery. For obvious reasons, the Southern Church would prefer to be remembered for its support of the "Spirituality of the Church" rather than slavery, much like southerners insist they fought for "States' Rights." The degree to which this is true for each is still hotly debated. For understandable reasons, those on the "right side of history" have never fully accepted that support for and the preservation of the institution of slavery might not have been a primary motivation for many, and thus, those on the wrong side will forever bear a stigma, regardless of their motivations for secession or division. But the question is worthy of consideration whether many in the Southern Church, and especially in border states like West Virginia, were more motivated by the Spirituality Doctrine than the slavery question. The answer, at least as it pertains to West Virginia, can be explored through four interwoven points: 1) West Virginia generally supported the Union; 2) the Presbyterian Church in West Virginia generally disfavored slavery; 3) nevertheless, the Presbyterian Church in West Virginia generally adhered to the Southern Church; and 4) the examples of three specific church splits may illustrate that ecclesiastical concerns overshadowed support for slavery.

West Virginia's Support for the Union

With the exception of some counties closest to Virginia, West Virginia generally supported the Union. The reasons were mostly secular: "Decades of underrepresentation in the Virginia legislature, a lack of state funding for education and roads, and a relatively small slave population encouraged this sentiment. So did commercial ties to western Pennsylvania and eastern Ohio."[8] Voter turnout for West Virginia's 1861 statehood referendum (35 percent) was disappointingly low, possibly because, with a war going on, "the people have too much else to think about." Nevertheless the vote was definitive, as 18,408 supported division and only 781 opposed it.[9]

The vote for the new constitution followed shortly after, and support was likewise overwhelming, with 18,862 for and 514 against.[10] It must be noted, however, that no vote on the constitution was recorded in twelve counties, most of which were southernmost or geographically linked to East Virginia.[11] Perhaps southern allegiances disinclined their citizens to participate or political shenanigans prevented it. Given West Virginia's history of political intrigue (as the well-known story of the State's creation illustrates), shenanigans would not have been surprising.[12] The end result of it all, though, was the successful creation of a new state and constitution, ostensibly with overwhelming public support.

---

[8] Stanley Harold, *Border War: Fighting over Slavery before the Civil War* (Chapel Hill NC: The University of North Carolina Press, 2010), 201.

[9] "The Election Today: Statehood Referendum, *Wheeling Daily Intelligencer* October 24, 1861," *West Virginia Department of Arts, Culture, and History*, Accessed March 21, 2019, www.wvculture.org.

[10] "Vote Totals by County on the West Virginia State Constitution April 3, 1862," *West Virginia Department of Arts, Culture, and History*, Accessed March 21, 2019, www.wvculture.org.

[11] The southernmost counties were Wyoming, and McDowell. These were also among the poorest and most secluded. Webster, Greenbrier, Pocahontas, and Monroe comprised the well-travelled river valleys just west of the Alleghenies. East of the Alleghenies were Morgan, Jefferson, Berkeley, and Frederick (VA). Fayette county contained the Midland Trail, a major thoroughfare between Greenbrier and Kanawha. The outlier Lewis was in the middle of the state, even though other nearby counties in each of these regions managed to participate.

[12] For a discussion of how the "circumstances of [West Virginia's] admission leaves doubt as to whether the granting of statehood to West Virginia had a basis in law," see Sheldon Winston, "Statehood for West Virginia: An Illegal Act?" *West Virginia History* 30, no. 3 (April 1969): 530-534.

Public support was especially strong in Malden, the home of the Kanawha Salines Presbyterian Church, where townsfolk had voted 238 to thirty-six to remain with the Union. In the later vote for the new state's constitution, the entire county of Kanawha had voted 909 to four in favor. As a hometown hero, Henry Ruffner's public support for the Union was probably heavily weighted by his people. He had personally delivered his persuasive "Union Address" in Malden in 1856, garnering some national attention. Likewise, the opinions of his brother Lewis—an elder in the church, community leader, and Kanawha delegate to the Restored Government of Virginia—probably also carried significant weight. The fact that his family business—the saltworks—relied so heavily upon slave labor makes his support for the Union especially poignant. If not a significant influence, he at least represented Presbyterian sentiments in Malden and Kanawha County. Assuming a normal distribution of votes in the nearly unilateral success of all pro-Union measures, it may be presumed that the Kanawha Salines Church also overwhelmingly supported the Union.

On the other hand, the Rev. Dr. John McElhenny demonstrates that some Presbyterians did in fact support the Confederacy, but with the important caveat that "he would fain have seen [slavery] abolished without bloodshed."[13] His county had not participated in the State Referendum for division, perhaps due to the aforementioned "shenanigans" or possibly because it had already voted for secession from the Union. But even in his own Greenbrier congregation, support for the Confederacy was not a given. One of his elders was Samuel Price, who voted against secession from the Union as a delegate to the Virginia Secession Convention of 1861, and who later served as a Lt. Governor in the Unionists' Restored Government of Virginia. Perhaps demonstrating a sort of solidarity, pro-confederate McElhenney once told Governor Price's wife, "These young people, who are rushing into this conflict with

---

[13] *Recollections*, 170.

so much enthusiasm, do not know what a calamity has overtaken us, or what tribulation we may have to pass through."[14] McElhenney was obviously grieved that tensions had exploded into war, particularly in the fields, farms, and families of his adopted hometown.

Lewisburg traded hands during the war, overrun by alternating armies. In September 1861, General Lee and ten thousand Confederate soldiers marched through Lewisburg on their way to confront General Rosencrans's army under General Cox, only to withdraw later as winter approached.[15] Then during Union passage through town, soldiers took over homes, churches, and schools, camped in crop fields, and slaughtered local livestock to feed hungry thousands. They even coopted McElhenney's beloved Donum, the steed which had borne him for years on his preaching tours throughout his expansive parish.

On May 23, 1862, the Union army decisively won the Battle of Lewisburg. According to Fry, "the citizens were refused permission to bury the Confederate dead. The bodies were laid out in the church until a trench, some fifty feet long, was dug, and in this enormous grave, without ceremony, they were laid away." When the war was over, ninety-five bodies were eventually reinterred in a grave formed in the shape of a large cross some 400 yards west of the Old Stone Church.[16] As the community's most venerated minister, McElhenney would have presided over this mass burial.

As personal as these affronts were, McElhenney's greatest personal loss was his grandson, who died at the Battle of Manassas in July of 1861. His assistant during this time, John Calvin Barr, wrote that "he always prayed for the return of peace, and that God would overrule the present conflict for his glory and the advancement of the kingdom of Christ."[17]

---

[14] *Recollections*, 170.

[15] *Recollections*, 178.

[16] *Recollections*, 179-180. This Confederate Cemetery can still be visited today.

[17] *Recollections*, 170.

Despite their loyalty to the Confederacy, Dr. and Mrs. McElhenney remained generous and gracious hosts to both sides throughout the war. Their granddaughter, a witness to all these events, wrote,

> The men and officers who visited his home were treated with impartial hospitality. From a general to a private soldier, their wants were supplied—their horses stabled, their owners fed and lodged. The chaplain of a northern regiment slept for several nights under his roof, thus protecting us from depredation.[18]

McElhenney was one of the exceptions to the rule in West Virginia—that the state generally supported the Union—though he was far from alone. However, Ruffner's position was more representative or influential overall, especially further up and further in, as reflected in geographical vote tallies and the overall success of the secession from Virginia. West Virginia's path toward statehood was highly irregular or, some have even argued, illegal. Nevertheless, it was democratic, and it could not have happened without a majority of the popular vote. In the face of this, and despite his Confederate allegiance, McElhenney did not believe the "peculiar institution" itself was worth fighting for. His reasons for supporting the Confederacy therefore must have been other than the preservation of slavery. And if Ruffner and his brother Lewis were also representative of Presbyterians in the State of West Virginia, it is possible to suggest that West Virginia Presbyterianism generally leaned toward the Union as well. At least it did not lean toward the preservation of slavery for slavery's sake.

Slavery Disfavored among West Virginia Presbyterians

The existence of both Union and Confederate Presbyterians and their lack of moral or biblical public arguments against the institution of slavery—regardless of their loyalty—could be interpreted as ambivalence toward slavery among West Virginia Presbyterians.

---

[18] *Recollections*, 183. Fry describes the chaplain as obnoxious and presumptuous.

However, the fact that Presbyterians of both allegiances continued in the Southern Church while at the same time engaging in private and public behaviors inconsistent with support for slavery indicates that this apparent ambivalence was rooted more strongly in the developing doctrine of the Spirituality of the Church than in any personal disinterest, confusion, or agreement with the practice of slavery.

By the time Northern and Southern tensions over slavery were starkly manifesting across the nation, the voice of Christian abolitionism had been around long enough to evoke the possibility that, in some sense at least, the Southern Church was "without excuse"—to borrow the language of Romans. William Wilberforce's work to end slavery in the British Empire was common knowledge. Among the Presbyterians, men like Alexander McCleod (a minister of the Reformed Presbyterian Church) publicly proclaimed that slavery was evil. His treatise *Negro Slavery Unjustifiable* was printed in 1802 and forcefully demonstrated that "the practice of enslaving our fellow men stands equally opposed to the general tenor of the sacred scriptures."[19] In *Presbyterians and American Culture: A History,* Bradley Longfield records that in 1818, "the General Assembly condemned slavery 'as a gross violation of the most precious and sacred rights of human nature; as utterly inconsistent with the law of God...and as totally irreconcilable with the spirit and principles of the Gospel of Christ.'"[20]

But among Old School Presbyterians in the border states, decades of opposition to the New School's secular agenda had driven them away from political involvement in any ecclesiastical capacity, at least in theory. They believed the Church had little business

---

[19] Alexander McLeod, *Negro Slavery Unjustifiable: A Discourse* (New York: T. & F. Swords, 1802). PCA Historical Center spotlights McLeod's work at "Alexander McCleod's Stand Against Slavery," *PCA Historical Center,* Accessed March 21, 2019, www.pcahistory.org. Noll surveys antebellum publications and arguments against slavery in *The Civil War as a Theological Crisis,* 39-48.
[20] (Louisville KY: Westminster John Knox Press, 2013), 87.

intruding into public issues unaddressed by Scripture, whether from individual pulpits or by the denomination as a whole. Preaching against one side for the other was viewed to be an unseemly contravention of the Church's spirituality. Personal beliefs among ministers varied of course, but generally speaking, West Virginia ministers of the ante-bellum era did not actively support slavery, even if they did not preach against it.

This apparent contradiction between personal beliefs and public inaction illustrates the development of the Old School/Southern Church Spirituality Doctrine. Consistent with this, Presbyterian ministers who continued with the Southern Church seem to have demonstrated their varied political loyalties mostly in their capacities as private citizens, rather than as ministers of the Word and Sacrament. At any rate, they did not favor slavery. Both John McElhenney and Henry Ruffner are cases in point.

A Case in Point: The Rev. John McElhenney

As has been said, John McElhenney of Greenbrier County was decisively inclined toward the Confederacy. He was a transplant, born and raised in South Carolina, which might explain some of his personal animosity toward the North. But Greenbrier County as a whole sent its sons to fight for the Confederacy, a fact for which McElhenney's migrant status and personal influence can hardly be blamed. In his capacity as a citizen, he nursed the Confederate sick, constantly visited their troops, and brought them "generous loaves of bread, hot coffee, and tissanes [tea]" prepared by his wife. However, in his capacity as a minister, he refused to address political issues (i.e., slavery) from the pulpit. He even refused to vote in local elections due to the prevalence of politicians in his church. In what can only be said to be an application of the Spirituality Doctrine, he did not "believe in the mingling of church and state" or in "introducing politics into the pulpit under the guise of religion."[21] Thus, he "never meddled with the slavery question."[22]

However, McElhenney's personal beliefs concerning slavery led him to free his own slaves many years before the war, only to hire them back on as free persons and at a "fair wage." Like many in his day, he did not believe slavery to be "unbiblical," but unlike positive biblical doctrines, he also did not believe it to be worth dying for. Instead, "he was interested in the society for colonizing the blacks in Liberia," a surprising reference to the northern abolitionist *American Colonization Society*.[23] Regardless, it seems his own conscience would not permit him to personally continue the practice. McElhenney's testimony thus illustrates the apparent contradiction of some West Virginia Presbyterians—allegiance toward the Confederacy partnered with a personal distaste for slavery. McElhenney clearly favored the doctrine of the Spirituality of the Church, however, and his church and presbytery joined the Southern Church upon its secession from the Northern Church.

Another Case in Point: The Rev. Henry Ruffner

Henry Ruffner, although transplanted to Lexington, Virginia, from his hometown of Malden, was a native-son of Kanawha County who maintained lifelong ties with his church, family, friends, and fellow-citizens of Kanawha. He visited frequently and returned there upon his retirement to once again serve the Kanawha Salines Church. As a private citizen, his Union loyalties and personal hatred for slavery were powerful enough to influence the division of the state from Virginia and the language of the new constitution. But since he was a minister, he was careful to frame his public arguments against slavery in mostly secular terms, almost to the point of raising

---

[21] *Recollections*, 168.
[22] *Recollections*, 64.
[23] *Recollections*, 170.

questions, to present readers at least, about his Christian beliefs on the issue. He even resigned his position as president of Washington College, lest his public positions risk being interpreted as ministerial and institutional endorsements.

In his 1857 pamphlet *Address to the People of West Virginia* (which was one of the first national publications to popularize the future name of the State),[24] Ruffner did not ground his argument in Scripture or morality as a minister could, though readers might infer from his language and tone that he believed slavery to be immoral. It seems his goal was to appeal to self-interest, perhaps because he understood that self-interest motivates more easily than altruism.

His arguments were not so much that slavery was bad for slaves, but that it was bad for West Virginians. Whites in East Virginia were outnumbered by and utterly dependent upon black slaves ("Their slave population is relatively eight times as large as ours"). For this reason, the legislature could not afford to take the distinct needs of West Virginia into account. He listed countless examples in support of this thesis, one of which was that West Virginia had been repeatedly denied funds for the improvement of roads that would have benefited the entire Commonwealth. Most pages of his address are taken up with statistical surveys demonstrating that Southern states were falling behind the Northern States in "progress of population," agriculture, manufacturing, iron-making, commerce, navigation, and education. East Virginia was therefore a slave to slavery, and it was killing the Commonwealth. Ruffner argued that all those states in which whites still outnumbered African Americans had best end slavery before the "deleterious institution" grew to a point of dependency and danger. To that end, Ruffner proposed a six-point plan for the gradual emancipation of slaves in West Virginia.

---

[24] According to historian Larry Rowe. Personal email, January 14, 2019.

His plan possibly influenced the language of the new State Constitution in 1863, but before it could be implemented, West Virginia abolished slavery outright in 1865.

Ruffner's testimony therefore illustrates the apparent contradiction of some West Virginia Presbyterians. Unlike McElhenney, he supported the Union and held a far more public stance against slavery. But like McElhenney, he retained his commitment to both the Spirituality Doctrine and to the Southern Church, even while disfavoring slavery.

Presbyterian Adherence to the Southern Church

Kanawha County had overwhelmingly supported the political division of the state from Virginia, while Greenbrier County, with its shared border and tighter Virginia connections, had lent its support more naturally to the Confederacy. This illustrates that location within the state indicated whether citizens were likely to throw political support to the Union or the Confederacy. Similarly, location within the state bore upon whether churches supported the Northern or Southern Church. Only Presbyterian churches in the northernmost counties continued with the Northern Assembly, while those in the eastern, central, and southern parts of the state adhered to the Southern Assembly. Thus it can be safely said that the Presbyterian Church in West Virginia overwhelmingly adhered to the Southern Assembly when the denomination divided.

In 1861, nearly 120,000 members of the Southern Church seceded from the *Presbyterian Church in the United States of America* to form the *Presbyterian Church of the Confederate States of America.*[25] To reduce losses, the 100,000 remaining members of the Northern Church presumptively acted to retain as many churches as possible in the border states. In 1863, Loyal Young, a minister in Butler County,

---

[25] *Lexington*, 104.

Pennsylvania (and later in Upshur County, West Virginia), presented the Northern General Assembly with a resolution to create a new presbytery in West Virginia:

> [Resolved,] that all the ministers in West Virginia, south of the south line of Pennsylvania extended directly to the Ohio, be detached from their respective presbyteries and formed into a new Presbytery to be called the Presbytery of West Virginia to meet at Parkersburg the first Tuesday in October next at 10:00 AM. . . . that any church or minister now belonging to other presbyteries in those States now in rebellion against the Government of the United States who desire from loyal feelings and motives to be detached from said presbyteries may apply to the most convenient presbytery adhering to this General Assembly and be received by them in virtue of this action.[26]

The extent to which the Northern Church expected this unilateral action to work is unclear, though it was audacious and optimistic enough to preemptively name the new presbytery after the entire state. Those locals in charge of bringing it to pass were at least deft enough to "send a circular to all the churches," polling which ones they could count on for support. The Clarksburg Church preserved its copy:

> Fairmont West Va. Augst. 18th, 1863.

To the Session of the Presbyterian Church at Clarksburg

Dear Brethren,

Whereas the General Assembly by its action of May 26th 1863 at Peoria, Illinois has recommended that all the churches of West Va. South of the Pennsylvania line be detached from their respective presbyteries and formed in the Presbytery of West Va. to be attached to the Synod of Wheeling, and as we are anxious to know whether it be expedient to form said presbytery, and what the prospects are, we send a circular to

---

[26] *Story of Presbyterianism*, 31; *Winchester*, 69.

all the churches proposing the following questions the answers to which we hope you will forward to us immediately.

1st What is the number of your membership at this time?

2d How many Elders have you in your session?

3d Have you a house of worship and what is its condition?

4th Have you a pastor or stated supply?

5th If not either how long since you had a minister?

6th Can you support a pastor if not how much could you raise annually in support of one?

7th Is your church divided on the national question and if so will your church organization—session and membership cooperate with the church adhering to the government of the United States?

8th Will you have a delegate at the appointed meeting at Parkersburg on the 1st of Oct. next?

9th Is your church in favor of the proposed new presbytery of West Virginia?

10th What is the number of scholars in your school?

Answers to the foregoing will enable those who go to or meet at Parkersburg to understand the condition of affairs and the wish of the churches, to judge of the expediency or inexpediency of organizing said Presbytery.

You can answer the questions on the same page and under the head of "Remarks" give such further information and views as you think proper.

Direct to Rev. J.H. Flanagan, Fairmont, Marion County, West Va., and much obliged.

Yours fraternally,

J.H. Flanagan

E.B. Hall[27]

---

[27] This letter is contained in the Church's session books at or about the date of the letter. The session recorded the following answers: first, 80; second, 4; third and

Unfortunately for the Northern Assembly, only five churches (including Clarksburg) sent representatives to that first meeting of the Presbytery of West Virginia, and its first meager report to the next Northern Assembly listed only eight West Virginia churches from Lexington (4), Greenbrier (2), and Redstone (2) presbyteries.[28] Northern connections and northcentral locations probably explain their readiness to abscond. Another two from Lexington joined soon after. The new presbytery then boldly claimed two additional, non-consenting Lexington churches (in Randolph and Pocahontas Counties) by placing them on its rolls peremptorily.

Concerning the loss of its churches, the Greenbrier's historian simply notes that "at that time, Parkersburg and other points transferred their connection to the Presbytery of West Virginia in the Northern Church."[29] On the other hand, the Lexington Presbytery immediately contested that the Northern Church had "claimed all the churches [in West Virginia] and actually enrolled them in the new Presbytery of West Virginia without their consent."[30] It may seem strange that Lexington was once again involved in West Virginia matters, but it has been previously mentioned that Greenbrier returned a sizable number of its northernmost counties to Lexington in 1858, on the grounds that it lacked the resources to properly evangelize them.[31] Thus Lexington was still active in West Virginia and stubbornly refused to relinquish its churches. The contested churches remained on the rolls of both presbyteries until 1869, when the Northern Church partially changed its posture toward the Southern Church. At that point, the West Virginia Presbytery removed the two non-consenting churches from its rolls

---

fourth, no answer; fifth, 1855; sixth, 300; seventh, "Dont know;" eighth, yes; ninth, yes; tenth, 40.

[28] *Story of Presbyterianism*, 31.

[29] *Greenbrier*, 28. Parkersburg, Hughes River, Mingo, French Creek and Bethel were all Greenbrier churches. The rest were either Redstone or Lexington Churches.

[30] *Lexington*, 125.

[31] *Lexington*, 110; *Greenbrier*, 26

(Mingo and Tygarts Valley in Randolph and Pocahontas Counties), and Lexington responded by promptly disenrolling six of its recalcitrant churches: Buckhannon, French Creek, Bethel, West Fork, Glenville, and Clarksburg. The churches that had willingly left Greenbrier and Redstone continued with the new Northern presbytery uncontested.[32]

Lexington remained embittered. For decades following, it refused "all movements leading to union with the Northern church." In 1887, they warned the General Assembly "that any Movement in the direction of organic union will create or foster division of Sentiment in our Church."[33] Tensions between the presbyteries did ease until representatives met in Clarksburg in 1889 to hammer out clear territorial boundaries for each. Both presbyteries and their respective assemblies agreed that the Parkersburg branch of the Baltimore and Ohio Railroad would officially mark the latitudinal boundary between the two denominations in West Virginia.[34] This agreement placed most of the state squarely within the bounds of the Southern Church.

---

[32] *Lexington*, 125, 415-16. The counties Greenbrier transferred to Lexington in 1858 were Pocahontas (north of Huntersville), Upshur, Lewis, Randolph, Tucker, and Gilmer. In 1860 Barbour, Harrison, Doddridge, and Tucker were also transferred to Lexington from Redstone (for some unknown reason, Tucker had apparently been previously listed in both Greenbrier and Redstone). The French Creek and Bethel churches of Upshur and Lewis were not originally a part of the transfer from Greenbrier, but Lexington placed them on their rolls anyway until releasing them to the West Virginia Presbytery in 1869. In 1858, the other two churches in Lewis and Upshur counties (Buckhannon and West Fork) were ostensibly returned to Greenbrier Presbytery, but Lexington also appears to have kept them on its rolls until 1869. The churches that originally left for the new presbytery were Morgantown in Monongalia County (formerly from Redstone Presbytery), Fairmont in Marion County (from Redstone), Bethel in Lewis County (from Lexington), French Creek and Buckhannon in Upshur (both of Lexington), Parkersburg in Wood (from Greenbrier), Clarksburg in Harrison (Lexington), and Hughes River in Ritchie County (Greenbrier). Glenville and West Fork in Gilmer and Lewis Counties (both Lexington) later joined their ranks. My conclusion that the West Virginia Presbytery "returned" Mingo and Tygarts Valley to Lexington is based on a process of elimination.

[33] *Lexington*, 126.

[34] *Greenbrier*, 35; *Lexington*, 126.

Even though the Northern Church had successfully resorbed a few West Virginia churches, the largest presbyteries in the state— Lexington, Winchester, and Greenbrier—remained whole-heartedly committed to the Southern Church. Given that so many West Virginians supported the Union and that Presbyterians generally disfavored slavery, the incongruity raises a legitimate question in modern minds: How could West Virginians support a denomination that explicitly labeled itself the *Presbyterian Church in the Confederate States of America?*

Whatever the motivations of ministers in other states, border-state support for the Southern Church is not always attributable to support for slavery. It has been noted above that the Southern church's unique ecclesiology was "born again" of Northern constraints, both secular and sacred, upon the Southern Church. These were tightest in the border states, where ministers experienced immense pressure to support the Union—their parishes were the border, after all, and the further south the Union could draw its lines, the stronger its military position would be.

Secular pressure came from tactics such as Major General William S. Rosencrans's *Special Order No. 61*, which required anyone attending a religious convocation to take an oath of allegiance to the Union.[35] Even Lincoln recognized such tactics to be beyond the pale, personally writing to Rosencrans to point out the contradiction "that while men may without an oath, assemble in a noisy political meeting, they must take the oath, to assemble in a religious meeting."[36] Religious pressure came in the form of the aforementioned Gardener Spring Resolutions of 1861, which had been the last straw for the Southern Church. Thus, considering the state's overall loyalty to the Union and disfavor of

---

[35] Graham, *Kingdom*, 50-54.
[36] "From Abraham Lincoln to William S. Rosecrans, April 4, 1864," Abraham Lincoln Papers, *Library of Congress*, accessed March 21, 2019, cdn.loc.gov.

slavery, West Virginia Presbyterianism's continuing support for the Southern Church suggests that its motivation was more concerned with preserving the sacred fidelity of the Church than slavery.

This preservation of sacred fidelity was one in the same with the Doctrine of the Spirituality of the Church. In *A Kingdom Not of This World*, Preston Graham uses the example of the embattled Dr. Stuart Robinson to show that Presbyterians in border states subsumed the Spirituality Doctrine as their own, irrespective of political loyalties or personal beliefs about slavery. By tracing the development of his convictions long before the war and their outworking during and after the war, Graham shows that the Spirituality Doctrine evolved independent of the social and economic contexts that precipitated the conflict.[37] In other words, the idea had been around long before slavery became an issue within the church. At the same time, Graham also shows how the border states were the first crucible in which real-world applications of the Spirituality Doctrine were tried by fire in America. Thus, in their high-pressure arena, Presbyterians in the border states may have led the way for the further development of the Spirituality Doctrine in the Southern Church and demonstrated that it was not "merely a post-war concession of [the Southern Church's] 'lost cause' theological realignment."[38]

Readers will remember from the previous chapter that Robinson was an adopted son of West Virginia, raised and educated in the Eastern Panhandle in the care of the Rev. James Moore Brown, and ordained to be the first pastor of the Kanawha Salines Church in 1841.

---

[37] The Spirituality Doctrine has its origins in the *Second Book of Discipline* produced by the Scottish General Assembly in 1578. Graham's thesis is that Stuart Robinson was connected to this tradition long before the war. See Kevin DeYoung's informative essay on the doctrine's history and value to the church today: "Two Cheers for the Spirituality of the Church," *The Gospel Coalition* (blog), January 31, 2019, www.thegospelcoalition.org/blogs.

[38] Graham, *Kingdom*, 169.

By 1848 Robinson had left West Virginia for Kentucky, where he pastored, taught seminary, and published a noisy religious newspaper called the *True Presbyterian.*[39] Under his editorship, the *True Presbyterian* brought national attention to the secular and religious pressures placed upon border-state ministers by the Northern States and Church. Though Robinson repeatedly asserted his personal loyalty to the Union, his newspaper loudly lobbied the Church to take a neutral position on the war. Viewing this equivocation as tantamount to supporting the Confederacy, the federal government seized the *True Presbyterian*, forced Robinson into Canadian exile, and, after the war, charged him with treason. He won out in the end, literally and figuratively, proclaiming that "he had faithfully maintained his integrity as a citizen of the United States and as a minister of a non-secular gospel."[40] After the war and in spite of his professed Union loyalties, Robinson continued with the Southern Church and was soon elected moderator of the PCUS General Assembly.

Robinson's story mirrors both the circumstances and the mindset of West Virginia's Southern Church ministers. West Virginia's overt support for the Union and secession from Virginia had not saved it from its own share of Civil War battles, particularly near the mountain range that separated West and East Virginia. The river valleys that crisscrossed the state had served as thoroughfares for troops from both sides to doggedly pursue enemies and vie for territorial control. A historian of the Tygart's Valley Church wrote, "In 1861, instead of the gospel messenger with the sword of the Spirit, our country was overrun by a relentless foe armed with sword and torch. Private

---

[39] Robinson published several periodicals during his years in Kentucky. Before the war he published the *Presbyterial Critic and Monthly Review*; during the war, the *True Presbyterian*; and after the war, the *Free Christian Commonwealth*. All three were mouthpieces for the Spirituality Doctrine that was being forged in border states. See Graham, *Kingdom*, 21-58.

[40] Quoted in Graham, *Kingdom*, 59.

residences, parsonages, and churches alike were invaded and destroyed."[41] As with Robinson in Kentucky and ministers in many other border states, West Virginia's ministers were in a straight betwixt two. None desired war, few supported slavery, many supported the Union, but most believed the Church should remain apolitical and free of state control. This dilemma led the largest share of West Virginia's pastors and churches to voluntarily fall in with the Southern Church.

The Implication of Three Church Divisions

Most of the state's churches survived the division of the denomination intact regardless of the assembly to which they adhered. A few did not. For instance, the Point Pleasant Church split in 1867, several years after the war had ended. Thirty years earlier, the church had declared for the Old School Assembly.[42] But during the years following the war, churches and synods were still aligning and realigning their Old and New School/Southern and Northern Church allegiances, particularly in the border states.[43] An 1867 congregational vote to adhere to the Northern assembly occasioned the official withdrawal of a Southern minority, although they may have been meeting separately for several years prior. Bitterness over slavery, defeat, or Reconstruction seems unlikely to have been a primary motivation for the withdrawal, given the town's pro-Union sentiments, its border with a strongly abolitionist state, and the church's age-old ties to the Gallipolis congregation across the river. It seems more likely that ecclesiological issues were at play, especially so long after the war and the resolution of the slavery issue. In the split, the Northern congregation took the building and property, leaving the "homeless" Southern Presbyterians to meet at a generous Methodist church

---

[41] Quoted in *Greenbrier*, 40.
[42] "Point Pleasant Presbyterian Church," Hall's Index of Churches, *Presbyterian Historical Society,* accessed June 18, 2018, www.history.pcusa.org.
[43] Graham, *Kingdom*, 173.

nearby. Nevertheless, the Southern congregation outlasted and outgrew the Northern. When the original congregation was compelled to dissolve in 1893, its remaining members reunited with the Southern congregation and became valuable contributors to the life of the church.[44]

Another church which did not survive intact was the Clarksburg Church mentioned above. Like the Point Pleasant church, its split occurred years after the war was over. Clarksburg, the reader will remember, refused to join the Old School Greenbrier Presbytery in the 1830s but opted to join the Northern Church's West Virginia Presbytery in 1863. Ostensibly, all had gone well in the decades following these decisions, except that in 1878, a sizable portion of the congregation petitioned the session to join them in uniting themselves to the PCUS's Lexington Presbytery. If the session refused, "we, with great regret, must announce our intention to go it alone."[45] The next meeting's minutes record that "on motion the clerk was directed to make out dismissal letters to all the foregoing, in form 'to take part in the organization of a church to be called the Central Presbyterian Church of Clarksburg, in connection with Lexington Presbytery.'"[46] In this way, the church lost most of its membership to the Lexington Presbytery of the Southern Church, thirteen years after the war's conclusion.[47]

But even more than the divisions of the Point Pleasant and Clarksburg Churches, the division of the Kanawha Church may illustrate that something more was afoot than the remaining sin of a

---

[44] *Story of Presbyterianism*, 71; *Kanawha*, 356-358.
[45] Letter in the Session minutes at or about February 14, 1878.
[46] Session Minutes, March 10, 1878.
[47] The Clarksburg Church struggled in the years following the division. Within two years, the session resorted to begging (and nearly berating) the remaining congregants for the funds necessary to keep a preacher in the pulpit. See Session Minutes, March 6, 1880.

lost cause. Unlike the previous two, this church had adopted a resolution during the war "that the Kanawha Church will not send delegates to Presbyteries on either side of this controversy."[48] Consequently, the congregation "was very nearly in the position of a congregational church" for about a decade.[49] A mid-twentieth-century historian of the First Presbyterian Church speculated that race and slavery played a role in this decision, even though he repeatedly bemoaned a lack of access to the Kanawha Church's records. After all, he speculated, the church had a long history on both sides of the slavery issue. Henry Ruffner was loudly opposed to slavery and was a "strong Union man." His family owned the slave-employing saltworks from which the church had indirectly benefited. Henry's cousin David served as a Lieutenant Colonel in the Confederate army. How could the national question not have played a major role in the division? The speculating historian, however, failed to explain the contradiction of church-elder and family-patriarch Lewis Ruffner's support for the Union as the owner-operator of the salt-works.[50] Such support would have inexorably ended the institution upon which his and his family's business had so long depended.

On the other hand, Gill Wilson, a minister-historian of the Northern Church in West Virginia, provided a substantial hint that more was at play than "rasped sensibilities and chafed emotions." Apparently he did have access to the Kanawha Church's records, since he mentions in passing that "finally, a resolution was adopted, saying that this church would become connected with the Presbytery of West Virginia, *so long as no measures contrary to our consciences be forced on us.*"[51]

---

[48] *Story of Presbyterianism*, 42.

[49] *Kanawha*, 118.

[50] *Kanawha*, 118.

[51] *Story of Presbyterianism*, 42. Emphasis mine. Once again, Gill Wilson's book looks to have been published from an incomplete and unedited manuscript, so it does not present this as a direct quote. However, his change from the third person to the first person in the last portion of the quote suggests that, in the portion I have

Wilson does not give a year for this resolution, but his chronology suggests that it was near the end of the church's isolation and around seven years after the state legislature had formally dispensed with slavery.[52] At that time, therefore, slavery was no longer a practice by which the Northern Church could antagonize consciences, leaving the reader to wonder what was. The circumstance suggests the "measures" of concern were similar to policies and practices that had driven the Old School and New School division thirty-four years before, when the church had unequivocally adhered to the Old School Assembly of the PCUSA.[53]

Nevertheless, Wilson says the resolution failed to resolve the congregation's conscience concerns and was followed by the church's division in 1872.[54] The method of division was interesting and unusual, as related by First Presbyterian's historian:

> The Session caused two rolls of the members to be prepared; or rather prepared the forms for the members to enroll themselves, separately, according to each member's wishes concerning Church courts. The rolls were placed in the Lecture room on March 14, 1872 and on April 26, 1872 they (the ballot boxes?) were opened in the presence of the congregation. One roll (ballot box) contained the names of one hundred and fifty-three members; these were they who elected to depart with the Synod of Virginia and with the Greenbrier Presbytery which had been erected in 1838. The other roll (ballot box) contained twenty-three

---

italicized at least, he was indeed quoting from church records. As a Northern Church minister, presbytery historian, and West Virginia Presbytery leader, he appears to have had access to records that others did not have.

[52] If Wilson's chronology was inaccurate, then this resolution could have occurred as early 1863, and slavery definitely could have been at issue as a matter of conscience. The Kanawha Church's records from this era—at one time "jealously shielded from the historian's eye"—now appear to be archived by the Presbyterian Historical Society in Philadelphia. I will publish any necessary revisions when I get the opportunity to review the records personally.

[53] "Kanawha Presbyterian Church," *Hall's Index of Churches, Presbyterian Historical Society*, accessed November 15, 2018, www.history.pcusa.org.

[54] *Story of Presbyterianism*, 42.

names; these were they who chose to remain with the Synod of Pennsylvania and the newly formed West Virginia Presbytery.[55]

The members of the smaller Northern congregation continued as the Kanawha Church, and the larger Southern group became the Presbyterian Church of Charleston (later, the First Presbyterian Church). They divided the property, allotting the smaller northern portion to the First Church, and the larger southern portion to the Kanawha Church. The secular courts awarded the records of the church to the Kanawha Church, implicitly declaring it to be the continuing church and the mother congregation.[56]

The Old Side-New Side Schism prepared the way for a unique Appalachian mountain religion by introducing and popularizing revivalistic pietism in West Virginia. It also provided for the establishment of alternative educational institutions that later perpetuated Old School theology away from the influence of New England Theology. This theology settled into the Southern Church as a reaction to New School religious agendas in secular contexts. Within the border states especially, the developing Spirituality Doctrine moved Old School Presbyterians to support the Southern Church, even when they personally favored the Union cause or disfavored slavery. West Virginia Presbyterianism exemplified this tendency, as illustrated in the specific cases of John McElhenney, Henry Ruffner, and the three divided churches. Thus, the strong possibility should be considered that, among West Virginia Presbyterians at least, adherence to the Southern Church was more likely about preserving the Spirituality of the Church than supporting slavery.

---

[55] *Kanawha*, 118.
[56] *Kanawha*, 119-120.

7

PRESBYTERIANISM AND THE AFRICAN-AMERICAN EXPERIENCE

THE INTERSECTION OF PRESBYTERIANISM and the African-American experience is a suitable topic for a book on Presbyterian history in West Virginia for four reasons: 1) Among the first people to bring slaves into the western waters were prominent Presbyterians. Slave-labor made them very wealthy and influential and benefitted the church. 2) Rev. Henry Ruffner's *Address to the People of West Virginia* was an important war-era document that made a case for the gradual emancipation of slaves within the territory of West Virginia. Understanding the historical context from which this influential document derives and to which it was addressed necessarily involves considering the black experience in West Virginia. 3) Virginia was rent in two when West Virginia seceded to join the Union. The previous chapter explained why most West Virginia Presbyterians then proceeded to adhere to the Southern Church, but modern Presbyterians should still face the ignominy suggested by the apparent contradiction. 4) The contemporary cultural milieu of church and society suggests that an honest review of the black experience among Presbyterians in West Virginia is appropriate and timely.

Slavery in West Virginia

As in the rest of America, the African-American experience in West Virginia begins with slavery. Slavery never inhered in West Virginia culture and society as it did in the east. Before the western waters opened, slaves only worked small farms in what is now the Eastern Panhandle. These were seldom as large as those of eastern Virginia, and landowners were not nearly as wealthy. West of the Alleghenies, in the main body of what is now West Virginia, the economy was not agrarian. The earliest pioneers struggled to provide for themselves, so few needed or could afford slaves. The result was that the slave population in West Virginia remained low in comparison to the rest of the Commonwealth. By 1860 slaves made up thirty percent of the eastern Virginia population, but west of the Blue Ridge, including West Virginia, slaves made up only four percent.[1] At that time, 6,823 slaves were concentrated in Hampshire, Morgan, Berkeley, and Jefferson Counties of the Eastern Panhandle. West of the Alleghenies, 1,114 slaves were put to work in the coal mines of Monroe County, 1,525 by the gentility of Greenbrier County, and 2,184 in the saltworks and coal mines of Kanawha County.[2] In areas where slave-leasing was popular, like Kanawha, populations varied from year to year. Nevertheless, Kanawha County always contained the largest concentration of slaves on the western waters.

The Kanawha Salines

Because the first commercial salt furnace of the Kanawha Valley was founded by enterprising Presbyterians, the African-American experience intersected with Presbyterianism early in West Virginia's history. Most readers probably do not know that salt—not coal—was

---

[1] "A Brief History of African Americans in West Virginia," *West Virginia Archives and History*, accessed July 1, 2018, www.wvculture.org.

[2] "African-American Population of Present-day West Virginia Counties in 1860," *West Virginia Archives and History*, accessed July 2, 2018, www.wvculture.org.

the first extraction resource broadly capitalized in the state. Coal merely fired the furnaces that dried the salt brine in the production process. Beginning in the early 1800s, salt production became the lifeblood of the Kanawha Valley. By the War of 1812, West Virginia was one of the largest salt-producers in the nation. Prices eventually fell as overproduction threatened to collapse businesses, but cheap labor and the innovation of trust-like consortiums kept the industry going for decades. "Cheap labor," of course, meant slave labor.

The salt industry required a massive labor force: furnace operators, coal miners, coopers, salt-packers, haulers, and loaders. Fully half of the slaves in the Kanawha Valley worked in and around the salt industry, and nearly half of these worked in the coal mines.[3] During the height of production, anywhere from one to three thousand were employed in any one year. Most were leased from slave-owners in eastern Virginia.[4] Leasing allowed salt barons to annually adjust the number of slaves according to production projections. The workforce was racially integrated, and African-Americans were paid for their work, but transient white day-laborers often left the hardest and most dangerous jobs to them.[5] To protect their investments, lessees and lessors took out life-insurance to recoup expenses when slaves were injured or killed.[6]

The Ruffner family features prominently in the history of both the salt industry and Presbyterianism in West Virginia. Around 1796, David and Joseph Ruffner moved with their parents and three siblings from a farm in the Valley of Virginia to the Kanawha Valley. There they built the first commercial saltworks on a 502-acre tract of land

---

[3] "Antebellum Slavery," *West Virginia Archives and History*, accessed July 1, 2018, www.wvculture.org.
[4] Cyrus Forman, *A Briny Crossroads: Salt, Slavery, and Sectionalism in the Kanawha Salines*, Master's thesis, City College of New York, 2014, 20.
[5] Forman, *A Briny Crossroads*, 9-17.
[6] Forman, *A Briny Crossroads*, 16.

purchased by their father, Joseph Sr., on the Kanawha River at Campbells Creek.[7] Others in the valley had dug and sold salt before them, and many more would do so after, but their innovations established them as pioneers in the industry. They were the first to drill (instead of dig) to reach deeper and more concentrated brines.[8] They invented the first commercial salt furnace in 1808. They innovated the use of coal instead of wood as a fuel for the furnaces, forming the leading edge of the coal mining industry in West Virginia.

As many other salt makers copied their innovations, the town of Malden grew up around the saltworks (on Ruffner property, no less) and became the "core of the commercial life of the Kanawha Valley."[9] Within a few years of Ruffner's first furnace, as many as fifty-two additional furnaces were producing millions of salt bushels annually.[10] The Ruffners became one of the largest landowning families in the region, buying up miles of property along the Kanawha River, from

---

[7] *Kanawha*, 59-62.

[8] J. E. Brantly, *History of Oil Well Drilling* (Houston: Gulf Pub. Co., 1971), 66ff. They pioneered the use of hollow logs to drill down to and pipe deeper and richer brines. A detailed, near-contemporaneous description of this process is recorded in *Kanawha*, 65-67.

[9] *Kanawha*, 68. An example of a driller who copied the Ruffners was William Dickinson, who drilled his first well using the hollow-log method in 1817. The Dickinson family went on to establish the largest salt-producing consortium in the valley (and to become the largest slave employer). The Ruffner's saltworks was second in size only to the Dickenson's. The Dickinsons have Presbyterianism in their heritage as well, since much later Col. John Q. Dickenson (1831-1925) was an elder in the Kanawha Salines Presbyterian Church under the Rev. John Calvin Brown's pastorate (1867-1892). He was a Confederate war veteran who rescued the family's business after a disastrous flood in 1861 (*Kanawha*, 20). Recently, descendants of the Dickinson family have revived the business on the original family property as *J.Q. Dickinson Salt-Works*, producing "high-quality artisanal salt in support of the organic, farm-to-table movement." Tours are available. Their website overviews the history of salt in the Kanawha Valley and their modern organic methods, and apologetically addresses the history of slavery in the industry. See www.jqdsalt.com.

[10] By 1815 there were "no less than 52 furnaces in operation, and many others in course of erection; all within 6 ½ miles along the river beginning 2 ½ miles below the first well and extending 4 miles above" (*Kanawha*, 68).

below Malden all the way into downtown Charleston.[11] Some of this property would later be donated to the Kanawha and Kanawha Salines congregations.

David Ruffner

In testimony to Ruffner influence upon Presbyterianism in the valley, the First Church of Charleston credits Ruffner-family heritage to "seven strong and influential Presbyterian Churches and two or three presbyteries in the Synod of West Virginia."[12] Colonel David Ruffner (1767-1843) was the progenitor of this heritage. With his "superior intellect, genial disposition, and generous nature," Colonel Ruffner was once "the most prominent and the most influential man in the Kanawha Valley."[13] Under Ruffner's leadership, "salt was king...and while the dynasty prospered the cause of the Christian Church prospered also."[14] Histories do not focus on the fact that David's religion was inextricably linked to slavery, but both were quite literally a family heritage. To wit, David and his brothers were willed "a large Luther's version German Bible" and three slaves upon their father's death in 1803.[15]

David Ruffner's contribution to religion in the valley began when he opened his home to services for the *Society of Christians Called*

---

[11] David Ruffner built the Holly Grove Mansion in 1815, which now stands on the grounds of the West Virginia State Capital. A half mile west of the capital building on Kanawha Blvd is the former Ruffner Cemetery, now called Kanawha Rifleman's Memorial Park, where the gravestones of Joseph Ruffner, Sr. (1740-1803), his wife Anna Ruffner (1742-1820), and Elizabeth Ruffner (1769-1841), wife of Daniel Ruffner, are still visible. Over one hundred other graves were covered over when the cemetery was made a park in 1920 (the stones were laid flat and buried). As all this was once Ruffner property, the distance between the location of the saltworks in Malden and the house and park in Charleston demonstrates the extent of the Ruffner's landholdings along the river—more than five miles.

[12] *Kanawha*, 56.

[13] *Kanawha*, 68.

[14] *Kanawha*, 68-69.

[15] *Kanawha*, 61.

Presbyterians. He built "Colonel Ruffner's Meeting House" sometime after 1815 near the mouth of Georges Creek. He then donated land for the construction of the Mercer Academy, the Presbyterian Church on Kanawha in Charleston, and the Presbyterian Church at Kanawha Salines (Malden). The latter still meets in the building for which David Ruffner "oversaw every brick laid."[16] The "seven strong and influential Presbyterian Churches" mentioned above probably emerged by descent and division from these two churches and are in that way creditable to Ruffner benevolence.[17] Once his son Lewis took over the business, David "devoted his time henceforward to the religious improvement of the people of the valley."[18] However, like all the salt-kings of the valley and thousands of other Christians in the southern states, Colonel David Ruffner was still a slave-holder.

Ruffner family connections to the African-American experience continued and broadened through David's children, two of which took very different but influential tacks. His eldest son, Henry (1790-1861), organized those first two Presbyterian churches in the Kanawha Valley and then embarked upon a long career as a college professor and president. Youngest son Lewis (1797-1883) took over the saltworks. Both were slave-holders, but each made conscientious efforts to improve life for African Americans in West Virginia.

---

[16] Larry L. Rowe, *History Tour of Old Malden Virginia and West Virginia: Booker T. Washington's Formative Years,* (Self-Published, 2014). This pamphlet was self-published by local Malden historian, attorney, and State Delegate Larry Rowe, whose history of Booker T. Washington and Malden WV is forthcoming.
[17] My best guess is that these seven churches are Kanawha Salines/Kanawha Charleston (1819), First Charleston (1872), First South Charleston (1919), Bream Memorial (1898?), Ruffner Memorial (1919), Elk Hills (1942), and South Park (1946). The first two divided out and the last four descended from First Church of Charleston. All seven still exist today. Other missions or churches (such as Greenwood, Lick Branch, and Kanawha City) appear to have come and gone (*Kanawha*, 264-271).
[18] *Kanawha*, 71.

Lewis Ruffner

Major General Lewis Ruffner was remembered by Carter G. Woodson and Booker T. Washington as a man who tried in his own way to make life better for slaves (and later, employed freedmen) in the Kanawha Valley. In 1820, he was ordained an elder in the Presbyterian Church on Kanawha and at the Kanawha Salines. Though he remained a slave-holder until emancipation, *The Louisville Examiner* recorded that a few years before the start of the Civil War he actually joined an emancipation society.[19] Perhaps he was influenced by his Mennonite maternal grandfather, Henry Brombach, whose faith-tradition opposed slavery.[20] His most well-known positive contribution to the African-American experience in West Virginia was the 1865 donation of the land and materials to construct the first building of the African Zion Baptist Church of Malden, the mother church of the denomination in the state. In 1872, the church constructed a more permanent building that still stands in Malden.

Along with religion, Lewis Ruffner also supported African-American education in his community. Carter G. Woodson wrote, "About the only white person who seemed to give any encouragement to the education of Negroes at Malden was General Lewis Ruffner."[21] The Reverend Lewis Rice, founding minister of the African Zion Baptist Church, had started a school in his own home in Malden. The school later moved into the church and then into its own publicly-funded building. No doubt Lewis subsidized this work in some way, perhaps through donations or influence toward public funding.

---

[19] Rowe, *History Tour*, 2.
[20] Rowe, *History Tour*, 2.
[21] "Early Negro Education in West Virginia," *West Virginia Archives and History*, accessed November 16, 2018, www.wvculture.org.

Upon the ratification of the Ordinance of Secession from the Union in May of 1861, Delegate Lewis Ruffner and other community leaders voted unanimously to create the Restored Government of Virginia at the first Wheeling Convention in June.[22] Upon Abraham Lincoln's promise of protection, the Convention met again in August and proposed to form the new "State of Kanawha." In November, Lewis voted for the new state's constitution at the first Constitutional Convention (with a new name, *West Virginia*—the convention agreed that "Kanawha" was too hard to spell). The people of West Virginia approved the convention's actions in 1862. The state was officially received by the Union in 1863.[23]

With reference to African Americans in the state, the constitution at first said simply, "No slave shall be brought, or free person of color be permitted to come into this State for permanent residence." A year later, the Willey Amendment was approved as a replacement, by condition of the federal government. While the Emancipation Proclamation had freed slaves in southern states, it had not applied to the new State of West Virginia. The Willey Amendment provided for their gradual emancipation:

> The children of slaves born within the limits of this State after the fourth day of July, eighteen hundred and sixty-three, shall be free; and all slaves within the said State who shall, at the time aforesaid, be under the age of ten years, shall be free when they arrive at the age of twenty-one years; and all slaves over ten and under twenty-one years,

---

[22] "Delegates to the Second Wheeling Convention," *West Virginia Archives and History*, accessed November 16, 2018, www.wvculture.org.

[23] It was this process that led to accusations of "shenanigans" and illegality in the formation of the state. According to the US Constitution, new states cannot form from old states without the approval of both the new state AND the old state. Luckily, the Reorganized Government was also the only Virginia government recognized by the Union. So the Reorganized Government simply gave itself permission to form a new state, and the rest is history.

shall be free when they arrive at the age of twenty-five years; and no slave shall be permitted to come into the State for permanent residence therein.[24]

But in 1865, the state legislature abruptly abolished slavery, making the plan for gradual emancipation irrelevant. Lewis Ruffner's active participation in the process leading up to emancipation reveals that he was thoroughly committed to ending slavery in West Virginia.

Booker T. Washington

After emancipation in West Virginia, Booker T. Washington lived with and was employed by Lewis Ruffner and his wife Viola for a time. This fact probably underlies the claim that Washington sometimes sat in the former slave gallery of the Kanawha Salines church while attending services.[25] He may have even been catechized in the Presbyterian tradition by the Reverend Dr. John Calvin Brown.[26]

Washington was an emancipated slave who came with his mother to the Salines from the Valley of Virginia in 1865 at the age of nine.[27] Not unlike a slave, his step-father forced him to pack salt barrels for endless hours and then claimed his pay. The entire black community of Malden and many "degraded white people" lived in abject poverty "in the midst of a cluster of cabins crowded closely together, and as there were no sanitary regulations, the filth about the cabins was often intolerable."[28] Washington hated this life and desperately wanted an

[24] "Willy Amendment," *West Virginia Archives and History*, accessed March 21, 2019, www.wvculture.org.
[25] Rowe, *History Tour,* 2.
[26] Testimony of this comes from Brown's grandson, who said, "I recall the report that Booker T. Washington learned the Shorter Catechism from [Dr. Brown] on evenings in his kitchen" (*Kanawha*, 6).
[27] *The West Virginia Encyclopedia* (Charleston WV: West Virginia Humanities Council, 2006), s.v. "Booker T. Washington."
[28] Booker T. Washington, *Up from Slavery* (Garden City, NY: Doubleday and Company, 1901), 26. As a skilled image manipulator, Washington may not have been an entirely reliable narrator.

education that would move him beyond it. His situation did not improve when he took a turn in coal mines. A reprieve came when Viola Ruffner, Lewis's wife, hired him to be her live-in house servant. Of the nearly two years Washington spent with Mrs. Ruffner, he wrote, "The lessons that I learned in the home of Mrs. Ruffner were as valuable to me as any education I have ever gotten anywhere since."[29] Washington and Viola Ruffner remained friends until her death in 1903. Decades later, through joint reunions and shared memorials, the Washington and Ruffner families still attempt to maintain their historical ties.

In his autobiography *Up from Slavery*, Washington recounted an anecdote for which he wished the elderly Lewis Ruffner to be remembered:

> I saw one open battle take place at Malden between some of the coloured and white people. There must have been not far from a hundred persons engaged on each side; many on both sides were seriously injured, among them General Lewis Ruffner, the husband of my friend Mrs. Viola Ruffner. General Ruffner tried to defend the coloured people, and for this he was knocked down and so seriously wounded that he never completely recovered. [30]

Henry Ruffner

Henry Ruffner has been previously introduced. Bearing his Mennonite grandfather's name, Henry was "a strong Union man" and likely supported his brother's involvement in the Reorganized Government of Virginia.[31] Sadly, he died in 1861 before he could see his dream of a slave-free West Virginia fulfilled. Many years before the

---

[29] Washington, *Up From Slavery*, 44.
[30] Washington says the white group was the Ku-Klux-Klan (*Up From Slavery*, 78), but it may have been some other similar group, according to Malden historian Larry Rowe (personal interview. July 5, 2018). Mr. Rowe said that Lewis Ruffner suffered a head injury and walked with two canes for the remainder of his life.
[31] *Kanawha*, 92.

war, he mounted public opposition to slavery in western Virginia from his platform as the president of Washington College. In 1847 he delivered his *Address to the People of West Virginia*, later to be printed as the famous "Ruffner Pamphlet."[32] On the title page of some versions, the author is identified as a slave-owner, presumably to make his arguments appear more poignant. His retirement from the presidency of the college followed soon after its publication.

No matter what anti-slavery sentiments either abolitionists or gradual-emancipationist may have expressed in the years leading up the Civil War, racial prejudice was common in both the North and the South. Ruffner was a gradual-emancipationist who strongly opposed slavery and supported the Union, but his writings make clear that he himself was guilty of the prejudices of his day. His judgment of slavery as a "deleterious institution" and as "a plague" and a "disease" is stated in terms of its effects upon the white population rather than upon the slaves, and some portions of his *Address* read as though he blamed the "evil" and "pernicious" effects of slavery upon the slaves instead of the slaveholders. He delivered another rousing "Union Speech" in his hometown of Malden in 1856, mentioning African-Americans only once: "It is only the African race, bond and free, who are of so different a type from the rest, that they cannot incorporate with the masses; but must remain ever distinct; not by the will of man, but of God who made us all."[33] Accordingly, the fifth point of his six-point plan to end slavery in West Virginia reveals his solution to this "deficiency" in the African race:

> Let the emancipated be colonized. — This would be best for all parties. Supposing that by exportation, our slave population should in twenty-two years be reduced to 40,000. Then about 1000 would go out free the

---

[32] (Lexington VA: R.C. Noel, 1847).
[33] Ruffner, Henry, *Union Speech; Delivered at Kanawha Salines, Va., on the Fourth of July, 1856* (Cincinnati OH: Applegate and Co., 1856), 11.

first year, and a gradually smaller number each successive year. The 1000 could furnish their own outfit, by laboring a year or two as hirelings; and their transportation to Liberia would cost the people of West Virginia 25,000 dollars: which, as population would by that time have probably reached a million, would be in average contribution of two and a half cents a head. This would be less and less every year. — So easy would it be to remove the bugaboo of a free-negro population, so often held up to deter us from emancipation. Easy would it be, though our calculations were not fully realized.[34]

Ruffner's resort to this utilitarian appeal reflected a belief in a "middle way" that could end slavery later rather than sooner, for the greater good of slaves, he supposed, and without violence and injustice against slaveholders. He strongly opposed the extremist tactics of abolitionists, believing they did more harm than good to both whites and blacks. He thus gave them a substantial share of his opprobrium in the pamphlet. In his concluding appeal, Ruffner requested that East Virginia simply leave West Virginia to make its own decision on slavery without interference: "We [already] have in practical operation, if not in perfection, the political incongruity of slave interest and free interest, which is feared as a consequence of the measure we propose."[35]

When West Virginia became a state in 1863 (two years after Ruffner's death), the new constitution included a plan for the gradual emancipation of slaves that resembled Ruffner's suggestions. However, before the plan could be seen to the end, the new legislature abruptly abolished slavery in 1865. The slaves of West Virginia may have been officially free, but it appears that the late Henry Ruffner would have been just as pleased that West Virginia was finally free of slavery.

---

[34] *Address to the People of West Virginia,* 39.
[35] *Address to the People of West Virginia,* 11.

Given Ruffner's language, tone, personal character, and convictions, the reader can hope that his pamphlet's practical arguments casuistically hid a more morally grounded conscience on the issue. Perhaps his immediate legacy hints that he did indeed have better reasons, and that he passed them on to be more clearly revealed in his son, William Henry Ruffner. Although originally ordained as a Presbyterian minister, William demitted to give his time to the cause of public education. When he was a minister though, he had strongly supported his presbytery's meager and unsuccessful efforts to start "Sunday Schools for colored people." When a newspaper ran an editorial saying that "We do not think any good can possibly result," Ruffner retorted that there were already "a hundred such schools this day in peaceful operation in the state of Virginia."[36] In 1876, W.H. Ruffner engaged in a rhetorical battle with his former classmate Robert Lewis Dabney over the issue of free public education for all, including African Americans.[37] He became Virginia's first superintendent of public schools, where he continued the battle to provide free education (albeit segregated) for blacks and whites alike.

The Presbyterian Church on Kanawha and at Kanawha Salines

The church that Henry Ruffner organized in 1819—the Presbyterian Church on Kanawha and at Kanawha Salines—left specific testimony in its session minutes to its particular intersection with the black experience in West Virginia. On March 14, 1819, on the very day that the "Kenhawa" church was organized, the new session examined and baptized into membership a black man identified only as "Adam." His lack of a recorded surname suggests that he worked as a slave, most likely in the saltworks or mines. On May 2 of that same year, Adam partook of his first communion. The session's records, comprising seventy dated entries

---

[36] *Lexington*, 132.
[37] *Lexington*, 122, 132-33. Also, the Rev. Zachary M. Garris's summary of this exchange is worth reading: "Dabney takes America to School: A 19th Century Theologian Predicts the Failure of America's Public School System," accessed December 21, 2018, www.teachdiligently.com.

from that day in 1819 until April 10th of 1936, contain references to at least thirteen other African-American members of the church during that period.[38] On October 16, 1829, "a woman of colour" named Daphne was baptized into membership and received communion. On October 17, 1830, "three persons of colour" named Anthony Barns, Milly, and Hannah were baptized and received into membership. On March 28, 1831, three more "persons of color"—Peter, Henrietta, and Winston—were baptized, along with Caroline, "an infant child presented by her Mother Anarchy." On May 22, 1831, "Anthony Banes [*sic*—this is probably the Anthony Barns mentioned above] (a man of colour) died suddenly Sabbath morning." On October 9 of that same year, Lemon, a "man of colour," was baptized and received as a member.[39] On May 11, 1833,

> It having been suggested that Peter, a man of colour, had, since his connection with this church, on one or more occasions, indulged too freely in the use of ardent spirits, the session convened for the purpose of examining the truth of said charge. And the said Peter appeared, and was heard in his defence; and it appearing to the satisfaction of the session that the charge to a certain extent was well founded, it was resolved he be suspended from communion with this church until he manifest a suitable penitence for his said offence.

On January 12, 1834, Robert Edrington, "a boy of colour" was baptized and became a member of the church. On December 20, 1835, "William Henry, the infant child of Aneta, (a coloured woman)" was baptized.

---

[38] These records were reproduced in Katie Bell Abney, *History of the Presbyterian Congregation and the Other Early Churches of "Kenhawha" 1804-1900* (Charleston, WV: First Presbyterian Church).

[39] Depending on whether or not *Lemon* was a common name, this Lemon may be the same one mentioned by Cyrus Forman in his Masters thesis: "He was a skilled, company owned slave and not leased annually by the salt companies." Because of this unique position, Lemon was financially able to purchase his own child from his master for the sum of $400 in 1856 (*A Briny Crossroads*, 23).

The names of these fourteen people intermix with the names of hundreds of presumably white members. The source gives no explanation for why it only references records from 1819-1836.[40] We can probably trust that the same pattern continued through any unavailable accounts of years that followed. But this record alone demonstrates that African Americans were admitted to some of the primary privileges of the Kanawha church—baptism, membership, the Lord's supper, discipline, Christian burial, etc. Sources do not reveal whether this was common in the larger church, but if Lexington Presbytery's testimony is indicative, it was not. Their historian bemoans that in 1860 "less than a half dozen churches in the presbytery had Negro members enrolled."[41]

Of course, these records do not testify to what discrimination might otherwise have occurred within the church, to say nothing of the miseries of slavery outside the church. The mere fact that the clerks felt compelled to note race smacks of prejudice, though it is ironic that such discrimination preserves a record we would not otherwise have. Three years after these records end, the Kanawha Salines church

---

[40] Though I can speculate based on information I found in other sources: James Moore Brown began his pastorate in 1837. When the church divided in 1841, Dr. Brown continued as the pastor of the Kanawha Church in Charleston. Records that began when he was installed must have stayed in his custody after the church divided. Then in 1872, the Kanawha Church divided again and produced the First Presbyterian Church. The Kanawha Church adhered to the PCUSA and First Presbyterian to the PCUS. In this split, the Court gave the minute books, which would have contained Brown's records, to the "parent church," deemed to be the Kanawha Church in Charleston. The denominational differences must have caused tension between the two congregations, which is why First Presbyterian's historian bemoans that the session of the Kanawha Church "shields them from the historian's eye with jealous care" (*Kanawha,* 120), and "it is regrettable that the record of [James Moore Brown's] pastorate in Charleston is not available to the historian" (104). It probably did not help matters that both churches claimed to be the original congregation (hence, "First" Presbyterian). These records are now archived at the Presbyterian Historical Society in Philadelphia, where they await study.
[41] *Lexington,* 110.

The interior of the Kanawha Salines Presbyterian Church showing the balcony that once served as a slave gallery. Some of the benches in the balcony are original.

completed the new building which still stands in Malden. Many of the people mentioned above probably sat in the slave gallery, looking out over their master's heads. Given what we know of post-war racial sentiments, we can assume that black members were still relegated to this balcony for decades even after their emancipation. Visitors today can sit in those same seats.

At the building's centennial celebration in 1940, former pastor (1907-18) Dr. J. W. Carpenter returned to deliver a retrospective. In his concluding remarks on the "spirit of the church," he reminded the congregants that the church was always known for its lack of class distinctions.[42] He congratulated the church's lack of distinction between rich and poor, literate and illiterate, culturally advantaged and disadvantaged. He boasted that bank accounts, genealogies, and college degrees never divided the congregants, nor did their lives prior to their lives in Christ. Instead, he said, "Both Philemon and Onesimus would have found a warm welcome here."[43] Philemon—astute readers will remember—was a slave master, and Onesimus was his slave. Though he assiduously avoided mentioning African Americans and the community's history of slavery, they were obviously on his mind. As has been shown, there is some truth to the minister's comments, but his congratulations do not register the ironic degree to which his church community benefited from slavery in its early years.

Presbyterian Attitudes Toward Slavery

Slavery was not limited to the saltworks of the Kanawha Valley. It must be acknowledged that even Presbyterian ministers in West Virginia owned slaves, particularly the earlier ones. John McCue was accused of beating his, although that charge was likely false. James Moore Brown once "executed a trust deed conveying a negro slave named Aggy and her three children to a trustee to secure John N. Clarkson in the payment of a grocery bill for the sum of $162.30; the debt was to be paid in one year."[44] Henry Ruffner, of course, was a slaver-holder. John McElhenney inherited his slaves through his wife's family. His

---

[42] *Kanawha*, 21.
[43] *Kanawha*, 21-22.
[44] *Kanawha,* 118.

granddaughter said they were "invariably well treated" and then gave their names: "Cherry and her children came to him through his wife; Martha, whom I remember, was also received from her father's estate. Commodore belonged to my uncle, who, having no use for him, left him on the farm. Of old Uncle Mat's origin, I am uncertain."[45] But the fact that West Virginia ministers owned slaves does not mean that personal convictions among Presbyterians of either allegiance were not changing. For instance, it has been mentioned that Henry Ruffner lobbied to end slavery and McElhenney freed his slaves prior to the war.

Like Ruffner, however, McElhenney was not free of the prejudice of his day. For example, his granddaughter reported his casual use of a common racial epithet, including a story that showed he almost reveled in his prejudice:

> An anecdote I have heard my grandfather relate more than once shows that the high-bred South-Carolinian was not prepared to abrogate the color-line. He was travelling by steamboat down the Ohio River, when he came into conflict with an abolitionist of pronounced views. A discussion of the race-question took place, and finally my grandfather inquired:
>
> "Would you eat with a n*****, sir?"
>
> "Yes," replied the abolitionist.
>
> "Would you sleep with one, sir?"
>
> "Yes," was the unflinching reply.
>
> "Then, sir, you are too much of a n***** for me," retorted the doctor, rising from the table, and pushing back his chair.[46]

Such a story threatens to disqualify the man from our modern esteem, though he had on all other counts shown himself to be the consummate Presbyterian. It is indeed a disheartening anecdote,

---

[45] *Recollections*, 64.
[46] *Recollections*, 64, 68.

especially since his proud rehearsal "more than once" reveals so much more than its content, which is bad enough. But if such sentiments disqualify him from any respect whatsoever, then the memorials of many champions from prior generations must also be cast down.

Still, the questions should be addressed, "What accounts for the behavior of these early Presbyterians in West Virginia? How are their views concerning slavery and toward the black race to be explained?" Before seeking an answer to such questions, one must first grant that no explanation can ever justify what was clearly sin. One must also grant that these ministers were not merely guilty by the imputation of the "sins of their day." McElhenney and others like him were fully guilty in their own right, "as the natural and proper demerit of their own sinfulness."[47]

To say then, grievously, that they themselves were slaves to the common prejudices of the day is not to excuse them, but to aim toward an explanation. They were influenced by Northern aberrations of faith and practice, secular and religious pressures from the North, widespread theories (in both the North and South) about differences between the races, and—for ministers outside some border states—the economic normalization of the institution of slavery in the larger Southern context. In the midst of these influences, the developing position of West Virginia Presbyterians toward slavery could be summarized as a strong commitment to an apolitical church, to Scripture as neither endorsing nor condemning slavery, and to the administration of slavery according to a Christian ethic. To this could probably be added support for the gradual emancipation of slaves, for their recolonization to Liberia, and for the eventual end of the unfortunate institution in the United States.

---

[47] To borrow a quote from Jonathon Edwards in his defense of the doctrine of original sin against John Taylor.

It is hardly redemptive to consider that, as tensions mounted and the Church began its falling out, few Southern Presbyterians actually preached that slavery was biblical. More common was the view that it was "not *un*biblical." As we have seen, some indeed preached it to be evil, but most others more passively granted that it was unfortunate or less-than-ideal, though not endorsed by the Bible as a positive doctrine. But since they granted that it was "recognized" by the Bible, it was to be biblically regulated and was not a proper subject for condemnation from the pulpit.

Having this perspective, some southern Presbyterians preached a "slaveholding ethic": Presbyterians owed slaves the gospel just as much as freemen; Christian masters should treat their slaves as they would want to be treated if they themselves were slaves; They must treat them as brothers in Christ within the same family; They should provide them every opportunity and encouragement to live obediently as Christians, especially by keeping their families intact; Masters should not prohibit and should even encourage and provide for their education to enable their own study the Word of God.[48] As an example of this ethic, the Lexington Presbytery passed the following resolution in 1845:

> Resolved, that all our Pastors & Stated Supplies, should consider the servants of the households belonging to their respective charges,…that Pastors should carefully inculcate upon Masters & Servants their relative duties;… that Sessions be enjoined to establish Sabbath Schools for the oral instruction of the colored people in every congregation, where it is practicable.…Let Pastors be careful to enforce upon pious Masters & Mistresses, that they are solemnly bound to use their best endeavors to teach the Gospel to their Servants…that the parties should be placed in circumstances, so far as practical, in which the obligation in the marriage covenant may be fully and faithfully discharged.[49]

---

[48] Longfield, *Presbyterians and American Culture*, 96-102.
[49] *Lexington*, 115.

This position is consistent with what is known of the practices of Ruffner, McElhenney, and other West Virginia Presbyterians, in spite of their racial prejudices. Once again, McElhenney's granddaughter reported that his slaves were "invariably well-treated," but that he did not believe slavery to be unbiblical.

This position was also consistent with that of West Virginia's own Stuart Robinson, presented through his weekly periodical the *True Presbyterian* and in his embarrassingly-named treatise *Slavery as Recognized in the Mosaic Civil Law, Recognized Also, and Allowed, in the Abrahamic, Mosaic, and Christian Church.*[50] As a leading proponent of the Spirituality Doctrine in the border states, Robinson believed an apolitical church could only address the state on topics affirmed in Scripture, and even then, it could say no more or less than what the Scripture said: "Thus, the *True Presbyterian* could 'recognize' slavery as it was believed to be recognized in the Bible but would refrain from recommending slavery as an American institution or from recommending the abolition of slavery."[51] Preston Graham points out that Robinson's choice of the word "recognize" was very intentional: "Robinson's point was that slavery was not necessarily inconsistent with Scripture, even though he was unwilling to argue, at least not out of his ministerial role, that it should be perpetuated as an institution in the American context as based upon Scripture."[52]

Though many today believe the Spirituality Doctrine to be an important and enduring development of the era, it cannot be denied that its particular application to African-American slavery was a serious hermeneutical error. Its fundamental flaws were 1) its failure to acknowledge that race-based, African-American slavery was in no way

---

[50] (Toronto: Rollo & Adam, 1865). Robinson wrote this after he had left West Virginia for Kentucky and while he was in exile in Toronto, Canada.
[51] Graham, *Kingdom*, 104.
[52] Graham, *Kingdom*, 116.

equivalent to whatever slaveries (Egyptian, Mosaic, Roman, etc.) may have been "recognized" and "regulated" in Scripture, 2) its blind focus upon exegetical particulars at the expense of the "general tenor of sacred scriptures," and 3) its failure to bring the Bible to bear upon the "dynamics of the American economy."[53]

That being said, it must be understood that this blind equivocation arose in a unique *Sitz im Leben*. The previous chapter suggested that the slavery application of the Spirituality Doctrine was fleshed out in the Old School and Southern Church in reaction to New School abolitionism, a movement perceived to be only loosely tethered to Scriptural authority. For instance, many abolitionists were willing to grant that Scripture affirmed some notion of the propriety of slavery but were also willing to cast this aside in favor of the more general authority of Common Sense.[54] On the other hand, the Southern Church viewed with great suspicion any arguments against slavery that dispensed with the authority of Scripture. Thus, the Southern defense of slavery through Scripture, whether as a positive doctrine or not, was tantamount to defending Scripture itself.[55] Even abolitionists who attempted to argue faithfully from Scripture were disregarded, their voices lost amidst the seculo-religious clamor.[56]

Regardless of the reasons, modern readers are still likely to find it inconceivable that Christians of the Civil War era could justify slavery using the Bible, especially since biblical arguments against slavery had been widely disseminated for at least fifty years prior to the war.[57] Mark Noll explains why these arguments often fell on deaf ears:

---

[53] Noll, 53. Noll discusses the race-based slavery equivocation problem on pp. 51-74.
[54] Noll, 39.
[55] Noll, 45-46.
[56] Noll, 31.
[57] Again, see Noll's rehearsal of these on pp 39-48.

Nuanced, biblical attacks on American slavery faced rough going precisely because they were nuanced. This position could not simply be read out of any one biblical text; it could not be lifted directly from the page. Rather, it needed patient reflection on the entirety of the Scriptures; it required expert knowledge of the historical circumstances of Near Eastern and Roman slave systems as well as of the actually existing conditions in the slave states; and it demanded that sophisticated interpretive practice replace a commonsensically literal approach to the sacred text. In short, this was an argument of elites requiring that the populace defer to its intellectual betters. As such it contradicted democratic and republican intellectual instincts. In the culture of the United States, as that culture had been constructed by evangelical Bible believers, the nuanced biblical argument was doomed.[58]

But Presbyterians were no strangers to nuance, and their theological method was among the most complex of the day. A few pages later, Noll adds a comment that might explain why even the highly-educated Southern Church ministers of West Virginia were susceptible to poor biblical arguments: "On the eve of the Civil War, interpretations of the Bible that made the most sense to the broadest public were those that incorporated the defining experiences of America into the hermeneutics used for interpreting what the infallible text actually meant."[59] Particularly in the border states, these defining experiences would have included some or all of Northern aberrations of faith and practice, secular and religious pressure from the North, wide-spread theories about differences between the races, and the economic normalization of the institution of slavery in the larger Southern context.[60]

In spite of Southern Presbyterianism's hermeneutical failures and misapplication of the Spirituality Doctrine, West Virginia Presbyterians

---

[58] Noll, 49.
[59] Noll, 50.
[60] Noll, 56.

remained generally committed to the gradual emancipation of slaves, to the eventual end of the unfortunate institution of slavery, and, until that came to pass, to the administration of slavery according to a Christian ethic. But their commitment to an apolitical church explains their lack of moral or biblical public arguments against the institution of slavery, and their defining experience explains why it could be sadly said of certain ministers they did not believe slavery to be unbiblical.

African-American Presbyterian Churches

The African American population in West Virginia has always been low relative to the population as a whole. Today it is only about 3.6%, but it was still only 7.8% when slave numbers were at their highest in 1850. After their emancipation in 1865, the black population dropped lower before picking up again as jobs became available in the southern coalfields. The 1940 census records the largest numbers of African Americans in West Virginia's history at nearly 120,000, but even then they were only 6.9% of the population (Table 4).

Participation in West Virginia Presbyterianism has always reflected this disparity. Not only are black Presbyterians few and far between, there have only been four predominantly black Presbyterian churches in the state, all of which were founded in the first half of the twentieth century. The oldest was organized in 1902 as Ebenezer Presbyterian in the town of Kimball in McDowell, the state's southern-most county. The second was founded in 1907 in the same county only five miles away—Whittico Memorial in Keystone. Both were organized by the Reverend John V. Whittico, a 1898 (A.B.) and 1901 (A.M., S.T.B) graduate of historically black Lincoln College.[61] In Bluefield, twenty miles to the east, another black congregation was organized in 1922— Edwards Memorial Presbyterian Church. The close proximity of these

---

[61] *Lincoln University College and Theological Seminary Biographical Catalog* (Lancaster PA: Press of the New Era), 1918.

Table 4 *African Americans as a Percentage of the Whole*

Census	Free	Slave	Total	Population	Percent
1790	612	4,668	5,280	55,853	9.45%
1800	526	7,172	7,698	78,592	9.79%
1810	1,278	10,836	12,114	105,469	11.49%
1820	1,412	15,119	16,531	136,768	12.09%
1830	2,167	17,673	19,840	176,924	11.21%
1840	3,033	18,488	21,521	224,537	9.58%
1850	3,082	20,500	23,582	302,313	7.80%
1860	2,773	18,371	21,144	376,688	5.61%
1870			17,980	442,014	4.07%
1880			25,886	618,457	4.19%
1890			32,690	762,794	4.29%
1900			47,499	962,800	4.93%
1910			64,173	1,221,084	5.26%
1920			86,345	1,463,701	5.90%
1930			114,893	1,729,197	6.64%
1940			117,754	1,901,974	6.19%
1950			114,867	2,005,552	5.73%
1960			89,393	1,860,267	4.81%
1970			66,804	1,744,116	3.83%
1980			65,051	1,949,644	3.34%
1990			56,295	1,793,477	3.14%
2000			57,232	1,808,344	3.16%
2010			63,124	1,852,994	3.41%

three churches in southern West Virginia testifies to the large influx of African-American rail and mine workers during the coal boom of the early twentieth century.[62]

The fourth church was further north, in Charleston. Olivet Presbyterian was founded in 1921 by W.W. Sanders, another graduate

---

[62] "From the turn of the century through the early 1930s, African-Americans made up between 20 percent and 26 percent of the total coal mining labor force in southern West Virginia." *The West Virginia Encyclopedia*, s.v. "African-American Coal Miners."

of Lincoln College.[63] Then the Rev. A. G. Anderson served as the first settled pastor until he resigned in 1927, after which the church languished and was completely dropped from the PCUSA's rolls in 1933.[64] The decline of the remaining three coalfield churches matches the coal industry's downturn in the 1960s and 70s. Whittico absorbed Ebenezer in 1966, and First Presbyterian Church of Bluefield (a predominantly white congregation) absorbed Edwards Memorial in the 1970s.[65] The PC(USA)'s Presbytery of West Virginia is now considering shuttering the only remaining African American Presbyterian church—Whittico—because its membership is simply not sustainable.[66]

The experience of an early nineteenth-century black missionary to West Virginia portended this outcome. John Chavis was a black Revolutionary War veteran and licentiate of Lexington Presbytery. The minutes of his 1800 licensure record that the presbytery "did & hereby do license him the said Jno. Chavis to preach the Gospel of Christ as a probationer for the holy ministry within the bounds of this Presbyn. or wherever he shall be orderly called, hoping as he is a man of colour he may be peculiarly useful to those of his own complexion."[67] The General Assembly then commissioned Chavis to the western waters in

---

[63] Apparently Sanders also served as the state librarian (1913-14) and state Supervisor of Negro Schools (1914). *Lincoln University*, 62

[64] *Inventory*, 49

[65] Ebenezer Presbyterian Church" and "Edwards Memorial Church," *Hall's Index of Churches, Presbyterian Historical Society,* accessed June 18, 2018, www.history .pcusa.org. See also Bill Archer, "After 25 years of service Reverend Dr. W.D. Hasty bids farewell," *Bluefield Daily Telegraph*, last modified August 17, 2015, www.bdtonline.com.

[66] Personal telephone conversation with the Stated Clerk on or about April 15, 2018. The PC(USA)'s *2018-2019 Directory of African-American Presbyterian Congregations* lists only seven members and no pastor. A note says, "Unfortunately our Ministry Committee [COM] is working to determine if this continues to be a viable church. The last few folks who have been asked to moderate the session have had no luck contacting the church." Accessed March 31, 2019, www.presbyterianmission.org.

[67] "Presbyterian Educator and Minister John Chavis," *Presbyterian Heritage Center*, accessed March 12, 2019, www.phcmontreat.org.

1801. While he was here, he frequently preached to mixed crowds and was well-received. Banks says, "His journal, kept during an itineration in Greenbrier and Monroe counties as he passed through on his way to Kanwaha, records, 'preaching to 200 souls, both black and white with such effect that they urged me to stay there and be their pastor.'"[68] But his time in West Virginia was brief—probably only a few months. Upon his return, he requested to be moved to a field with a larger black population. He eventually went on to some fame as an educator in North Carolina, though he was never granted ordination by the presbyteries in which he ministered.[69]

---

[68] Banks, *200 Years*, 31.

[69] Lexington, 80-81; Banks, *200 Years*, 30-31. The PC(USA)'s Presbyterian Heritage Center in Montreat NC is thus incorrect to claim that he was the "first ordained black Presbyterian minister in America." For a fuller account of Chavis see Earnest Trice Thompson, *Presbyterians in the South: Vol. 1: 1607-1861* (Richmond VA: John Knox Press, 1963), 207-208.

8

EDUCATION IN PULPIT AND PEW

THROUGHOUT THE PREVIOUS CHAPTERS, keen readers will have observed hints of education's key role in Presbyterian history. They will have noted that West Virginia ministers were highly educated, that they often started schools, and that there was some sense in which education encumbered Presbyterianism's progress in the state.

The long-standing relationship between Presbyterianism and education probably has Puritan and Scots-Irish origins. The Puritans brought their Continental emphasis on education to New England, and the Scots-Irish brought theirs to the Middle Colonies. They both held Reformed theology in common, which—with its focus upon "the sovereignty of God over all things, including civic behavior and institutions and the life of the individual mind"—called for an educated clergy who could, in turn, educate the population. Presbyterianism thus "required commitment on the part of its adherents both to obtain an education for themselves and to make it available for others in society."[1]

---

[1] D.C. Hester, "Education, Presbyterians and," in *Dictionary of the Presbyterian Reformed Tradition in America,* ed. D.G. Hart and Mark Noll (Downers Grove IL: InterVarsity Press, 1999).

An Educated Clergy

Since they were among the most educated in Colonial America, Presbyterian ministers were well-positioned to impact religion, society, and politics "far beyond proportion to their numbers."[2] While Presbyterian historians probably overstate their contributions to the disestablishment mindset of the Revolution and the republican principles codified in the Constitution, the Scots-Irish had a long-standing interest in religious freedom and Church independence. National influence, however, was not the objective of their commitment to ministerial education. They believed that "the continued existence of the Church requires a trained teaching eldership, and the prime task for the pioneer ministers in the new settlements was to seek out and train successors and fellow workers."[3] Education was thus necessary to preach, preserve, and propagate Presbyterian theology.

The Great Awakening presented a challenge to this commitment. New England and Europe hosted the most respected educational institutions, making them impractical for Presbyterians in the Middle and Southern Colonies. During Old Side-New Side Controversy, slightly more progressive (though wholly orthodox) Presbyterians began experimenting with alternative means to meet the rising demand for ministers. Experienced ministers took it upon themselves to educate candidates on their own. William Tennant started the famous "Log College" of Buck's County, Pennsylvania, paving the way for many other academies, colleges, and seminaries: Princeton College, Hampden-Sydney College, Jefferson College, Washington College, Union Theological Seminary, Western Theological Seminary, and others.[4]

---

[2] *Lexington*, 58.
[3] *Winchester*, 94.
[4] *Winchester*, 95.

Though the earliest of these were controversial, they demonstrate that the New Side never left off the traditional Presbyterian commitment to preparing candidates and preserving orthodoxy. By the time the Old and New Sides reconciled in 1758, concerns about the quality of the new schools had receded.[5] Their availability assured that revivalism and pietism would continue to predominate on the frontier, and later, their convenience assisted the consolidation of Old School Presbyterianism into the Southern Church.

Around 1811, "the General Assembly, after mature deliberation resolved, in reliance on the patronage and blessing of the Great Head of the Church, to establish Institutions consecrated solely to the education of men for the Gospel ministry, and to be denominated *theological seminaries of the Presbyterian Church in the United States of America.*"[6] Western Theological seminary later reproduced the Assembly's goals for this resolution:

> It is to form men for the Gospel ministry, who shall truly believe, and cordially love, and therefore endeavor to propagate and defend, in its genuineness, simplicity, and fulness, that system of religious belief and practice which is set forth in the Confession of Faith, Catechisms and Plan of Government and Discipline of the Presbyterian Church; and thus to perpetuate and extend the influence of true evangelical piety, and Gospel order.

> It is to provide for the Church an adequate supply and succession of able and faithful ministers of the New Testament; workmen that need not be ashamed, being qualified to rightly divide the word of truth.

> It is to unite, in those who shall sustain the ministerial office, religion and literature; that piety of the heart which is the fruit only of the renewing and sanctifying grace of God, with solid learning: believing that religion

---

[5] *Lexington*, 28-45.
[6] *Plan of the Western Theological Seminary of the Presbyterian Church in the United States of America: Founded 1825* (Allegheny PA: J.H. McFarland, 1884), 2.

without learning, or learning without religion, in the ministers of the Gospel, must ultimately prove injurious to the Church.

It is to afford more advantages than have hitherto been usually possessed by the ministers of religion in our country, to cultivate both piety and literature in their preparatory course: piety, by placing it in circumstances favorable to its growth, and by cherishing and regulating its ardor; literature, by affording favorable opportunities for its attainment, and by making its possession indispensable.

It is to provide for the Church, men who shall be able to defend her faith against infidels, and her doctrines against heretics.

It is to furnish our congregations with enlightened, humble, zealous, laborious pastors, who shall truly watch for the good of souls, and consider it as their highest honor and happiness to win them to the Saviour, and to build up their several charges in holiness and peace.

It is to promote harmony and unity of sentiment among the ministers of our Church, by educating large bodies of them under the same teachers, and in the same course of study.

It is to lay the foundation of early and lasting friendships, productive of confidence and mutual assistance in after life among the ministers of religion; which experience shows to be conducive not only to personal happiness, but to the perfecting of inquiries, researches, and publications advantageous to religion.

It is to preserve the unity of our Church, by educating her ministers in an enlightened attachment, not only to the same doctrines, but to the same plan of government.

It is to bring to the service of the Church genius and talent, when united with piety, however poor or obscure may be their possessor, by furnishing, as far as possible, the means of education and support, without expense to the student.

It is to found nurseries for missionaries to the heathen, and to such as are destitute of the stated preaching of the gospel; in which youth may receive that appropriate training which may lay a foundation for their ultimately becoming eminently qualified for missionary work.

It is, finally, to endeavor to raise up a succession of men, at once qualified for and thoroughly devoted to the work of the Gospel ministry; who, with various endowments, suiting them to different stations in the Church of Christ, may all possess a portion of the spirit of the primitive propagators of the Gospel; prepared to make every sacrifice, to endure every hardship, and to render every service which the promotion of pure and undefiled religion may require.[7]

Western Theological Seminary in Allegheny, Pennsylvania, was one such school. Founded in 1825, its 1885 biographical catalog lists over seventy pupils who came from or ministered in West Virginia between those years.[8] They were instructed by such well-regarded professors as William Swan Plumer, Archibald Alexander Hodge, William Henry Hornblower, and Benjamin Breckinridge Warfield.[9] In 1959, the seminary merged with the UPCNA's Pittsburgh-Xenia Theological Seminary to eventually become the PC(USA)'s Pittsburgh Theological Seminary.

Another college of great import to West Virginia was Liberty Hall Academy. The Academy was founded near Lexington, Virginia, in 1782 by the Presbytery of Hanover, with a long-term view to educating candidates. Liberty Hall Academy later became Washington College (following a generation donation from George Washington), and still later Washington and Lee University (after college president Robert E. Lee). Hanover named the esteemed pastor and academic William Graham as the first rector. He modeled the school's liberal curriculum after his alma mater, Princeton:

---

[7] *Plan of the Western Theological Seminary*, 2-4.
[8] *Historical and Biographical Catalogue of the Officers and Students of the Western Theological Seminary of the Presbyterian Church, at Allegheny City, Penna., 1827-1885* (Allegheny PA: Published by the Seminary, 1885).
[9] A complete list of faculty is on pp. 15-17 of the *Historical and Biographical Catalog.*

While Graham subscribed to the commonly held view that theology was the queen of the sciences and ministry was the noblest of professions, he also believed that the aim of the education he offered should be to provide the mind with a knowledge of truth. By acquainting his students with a broad range of subjects, he hoped to prepare them for any business in life.[10]

Students entered the academy as young as ten and progressed through ranks of grammar and upper classes. They continued at the college level by reading Horace, Cicero, Lucian, Xenophon, and Homer in the original languages before moving on to "arithmetic, the first six books of Euclid's *Elements,* trigonometry, surveying, navigation, algebra, and conic sections."[11] Finally, students studied philosophy, electricity, astronomy, geography, English grammar, literature, and logic.[12]

Although students could graduate with a baccalaureate degree, Presbyterian ordination required more, so in 1792 Lexington Presbytery commissioned Graham to continue their education through the rough equivalent of what would later become standard seminary education.[13] This only certified the post-graduate tutoring Graham had already been doing for years. Ministers such as John McCue and Benjamin Grigsby thus attended the Academy and then studied theology under Graham's tutelage. The next president was George Baxter, who tutored John McElhenny, Henry Ruffner, James Moore Brown, and many other West Virginia ministers.

Presbyterian ministerial training included not only education, but licensure and probation, the whole of which encumbered

---

[10] John M. McDaniel, Charles N. Watson, and David T. Moore, *Liberty Hall Academy: The Early History of the Institutions Which Evolved into Washington and Lee University* (Lexington VA: Liberty Hall Press, 1979), 26.

[11] McDaniel, *Liberty Hall Academy*, 24.

[12] McDaniel, *Liberty Hall Academy*, 24.

[13] *Lexington*, 80.

Presbyterianism's outreach on the frontier. Most presbyteries required a baccalaureate, two years of graduate tutoring, plus two years' probation after licensure.[14] They carefully supervised their candidates, choosing which college they would attend and subsidizing food, clothing, and tuition.[15] Candidates "under care" regularly attended stated meetings to report on their progress. Support was discontinued for those whose progress was deemed insufficient for a future in pastoral ministry. Following graduation and licensure, presbyteries commissioned probationers to designated fields to itinerate, evangelize, establish missions, and search for calls. The probationer system may have helped supply pulpits where ministers were lacking, but it was insufficient to keep Presbyterianism mainstream.[16] By the time candidates finally qualified for ordination, they might have been under care for eight or more years. Only after surviving this lengthy gauntlet could they return to their fields, assume a pastorate, and plant more churches.

An Educated People

Wherever Presbyterianism went, a school was sure to follow: "In the early 1800s, a school in every congregation was a part of the Presbyterian program."[17] Ministers sometimes taught in or started their

---

[14] In Winchester Presbytery as of 1820, licensure required four exams: 1) Confession of Faith, chapters 1-3, Latin, and Greek; 2) Confession, chapters 4 to 10, Mathematics, Geography, Natural Philosophy, and Astronomy; 3) Confession, chapter 11-18, Moral Philosophy, Logic, Rhetoric and Pulpit Excellence; and 4) the rest of the Confession, Hebrew, Church History and Government. (*Winchester*, 97).
[15] *Winchester*, 96.
[16] Woodworth lists six ways that, "in the lack of resident pastors, these early congregations were supplied with the ministration of the Word and the ordinances of religion" (*Winchester*, 43-45): 1) nearby resident ministers, 2) licentiates, 3) ministers on social visits, 4) itinerate ministers [i.e., revivalists], 5) synodical missionaries, 6) schoolmasters and ruling elders.
[17] *Lexington*, 82. Public funding for high schools in West Virginia did not begin until 1911. Woodworth traces the steps by which over the course of a century education transitioned from private to public funding: "1. All secular education was Church-related; 2. The State took over primary education and the Church continued with

own private schools to fulfill the Presbyterian educational mandate, cultivate ministry candidates, and supplement income. They were the best qualified for this in nearly every community—not only were they the most educated, they had gained teaching experience by tutoring younger students during their graduate studies. They set up shop in homes, churches, and community buildings, and their schools were funded by private subscriptions. Where schools were impractical, they started Sabbath Schools to teach pupils how to read and study Scripture for themselves.

East of the Alleghenies, Moses Hoge started Shepherdstown Academy in 1787, and the Charles Town Academy began under William Hill in 1795. William Henry Foote administrated the Romney Academy from 1824 until 1837 and later started his own Potomac Academy in 1850. Stuart Robinson taught at the Charleston Institute prior to his ordination. John McElhenney established his school shortly after his arrival in Lewisburg in 1808. His Lewisburg Academy became a feeder for Washington College, and many prominent West Virginia ministers received their education through this connection. Henry Ruffner was so well-prepared by McElhenney that he was able to complete Washington's compete curriculum in a year and half. Ruffner went on to teach at the new Mercer Academy in Charleston on property donated by his father. He then commenced his long career as an educator at Washington College.

Several of West Virginia's most prominent colleges have some Presbyterianism in their blood. From 1846-1851, Rev. Silas Billings taught at the Monongalia Academy, a predecessor of West Virginia

---

academies; 3. The high school supplanted the academy; 4. In the present stage the Church has relinquished all secular education to the State except for a few mission schools in neglected areas and limits itself to such college, training schools and theological seminaries as are directly related to its own program of such secular and religious education as is necessary to supply it with trained lay workers and ministers" (*Winchester*, 152).

University.[18] Rev. Nathan Shotwell, the pastor of the West Liberty Church, founded the West Liberty Academy, precursor to West Liberty University.[19] The Presbyterian Church of Huntington partially funded the construction of Marshall Academy (now Marshall University) in 1838 on the condition that its facilities be available for worship services.[20] McElhenney's Lewisburg Academy, after several changes of hands and names, eventually became Greenbrier College across from the Old Stone Church.[21]

But the West Virginia college with the purest Presbyterian pedigree is Davis and Elkins in Randolph County. After years of planning by Winchester and Lexington Presbyteries, Davis and Elkins began offering classes in 1904. Two U.S. Senators— namesakes Henry Davis and Stephen Elkins—made the project possible through significant land and money contributions. The school began with fewer than fifty students and initially operated mostly as a secondary school with only a few college classes. The program quickly expanded, and the first baccalaureate degrees were awarded in 1910.[22] Davis and Elkins College remains the only PC(USA) post-secondary school in West Virginia. Of greatest historical interest to Presbyterians may be the odd fact that the

---

[18] *Winchester*, 153.

[19] *Inventory*, 85.

[20] *Inventory*, 157.

[21] The war disrupted operations and the Lewisburg Academy was restarted in 1872 as the Lewisburg Female Institute. Over the years it experienced many more transmutations: The Greenbrier Military Academy was added in 1890. The Female Institute later became the Lewisburg Seminary (1911), then the Greenbrier College for Women (1823), and then Greenbrier College (1933). The Greenbrier Military Academy was briefly called the Greenbrier Presbyterial School in the early twentieth century, before becoming the Greenbrier Military School in 1920 (*Inventory*, 254-255; *The West Virginia Encyclopedia*, s.v. "Greenbrier College for Women" and "Greenbrier Military School"). Both schools ceased operation in 1972. Today the former campus of Greenbrier College houses the New River Community and Technical College, and the Military School houses the West Virginia School of Osteopathic Medicine.

[22] *Story of Presbyterianism*, 89-90.

college was a joint operation of *both* the PCUS *and* the PCUSA almost from its start:

> In the year 1908, there was consummated an arrangement whereby Lexington and Winchester Presbyteries donated to the Synod of West Virginia (USA) joint ownership and control of the college, and from that date the college came under the management of Lexington and Winchester Presbyteries of the Presbyterian Church in the United States on the one hand, and the Synod of West Virginia of the Presbyterian Church of the United States of America, on the other.[23]

For good or ill, education has always been a priority for Presbyterians. They affirmed their commitment to clerical education during the Old Side-New Side Controversy by exploring alternatives, founding more schools, and expanding the denomination's ability to supply more candidates. Education for the pulpit went hand-in-hand with education in the pew. Ministers started many Sunday Schools, presbyterial schools, and private academies. These academies sometimes grew into colleges, and colleges led to seminaries. Though this education emphasis has been a great Presbyterian hallmark, it has still greatly hindered the denomination's progress in West Virginia.[24] The reasons for this will be explored more fully in the final chapter.

---

[23] *Inventory*, 259.

[24] See Appendix B: Suggestions for the New River Presbytery of the Presbyterian Church in America

9

THE PRESBYTERIAN PROBLEM

DESPITE THE STATE'S SCOTS-IRISH heritage and centuries of ministerial effort, Presbyterianism has struggled in West Virginia in ways that mirror the struggle of the state itself. As the frontier moved west, the attention of the nation and the larger Church moved with it, leaving behind an increasingly isolated Appalachian people who developed eccentricities that were later aggrandized into the stuff of legend.

For the first half of the twentieth century, Appalachians were popularly called "Yesterday's People."[1] In 1965, Presbyterian minister Jack Weller "wrote the book" on the Appalachian people and gave it that very name.[2] With the best of intentions, Weller's unsound methodology unwittingly contributed to many damaging

---

[1] McCauley, *Appalachian Mountain Religion*, 482.

[2] *Yesterday's People: Life in Contemporary Appalachia* (Lexington KY: University of Kentucky Press, 1965). His influential work has been widely criticized as belonging to an outdated "Culture of Poverty" approach to sociological studies that encourages deficit theory. See, e.g., Dwight Billings, "Culture and Poverty in Appalachia: A Theoretical Discussion and Empirical Analysis," *Social Forces* 53, no. 2 (1974): 315-323. While Weller's thesis has been challenged, his conclusions continues to influence popular sentiment, suggests Wilma A. Dunaway, *The First American Frontier: Transition to Capitalism in Southern Appalachia, 1700-1860* (Chapel Hill: University of North Carolina Press, 1996), 334.

stereotypes. He divided the entirety of Appalachian society into classes (e.g., lower class, folk class, working class, middle class) and brutally critiqued them all. For example, he concluded the following about the lower class:

> This segment of society tends to exhibit many of the same characteristics everywhere. It is a pathological society in that it does not deal adequately with the problems of life. It is not a problem-solving society—in fact, it is a problem-creating society. It does not foster the human values of personal worth, dignity, responsibility and happiness. The persons within it have failed to make life adjustments of the most basic kinds, and these failures are perpetuated. Family life is such that attitudes and habits are fostered which almost guarantee defeat for its members, and these family habits are passed on from one generation to the next. This class creates the most problems—mental illness, alcoholism, drug addiction, and instability of character. Because the lower classes receive far less adequate care than other groups, persons sink even deeper. This class produces people who can work only in unskilled jobs are therefore increasingly unwanted by the American economy. The spiral goes down and down, each problem reinforcing the others. Most of these families, having a number of serious situations to face, any one of which would be difficult for even a well-adjusted, adequate-income family to handle.[3]

Weller's intentions aside, it is extremely difficult to describe or diagnose problems within Appalachian culture without devolving into stereotypes. What follows is a brief effort to explain "how West Virginia got this way," and then to show that, from the beginning, the culture of West Virginia and the prospects of Presbyterianism have travelled parallel tracks. Some generalities cannot be helped, but understanding the state's troubles in broad terms may shed light on the Presbyterian problem in West Virginia.

---

[3] Weller, *Yesterday's People*, 151-152.

The State of the State of West Virginia

The geography that once made western Virginia so difficult for Scots-Irish pioneers has continued to shape Mountaineer history and culture. The hills and hollers have formed an enduring identity and way of life:

> The geography of Appalachia has impacted nearly every aspect of life there. The early isolation caused by the mountains led to the development of distinctive cultures and types of speech. The terrain influenced settlement patterns and heredity. The land provided the means for survival--farmland, game, and later the trees and minerals that would become the basis for the area's economy. So throughout history, the mountains of Appalachia have shaped the lives of the people who live there—and such is still the case today.[4]

Though long a point of pride and source of identity, West Virginia's geography has also contributed to its dysfunction. A once-thriving, extraction economy has been buried alive under an explosion of technological advancements, competition, and regulation. For generations, abused, under-employed mountaineers have been covered with the rubble of poverty, low educational attainment, and geographic immobility. Incredibly, the survivors exhibit inimitable pride at every downturn—from decals on the rear windows of cars proudly announcing the occupant's relationship to a coal miner,[5] to a motto that declares that "Mountaineers are always free," to border signs that proclaim the state to be "Almost Heaven." Mountaineer pride endures beyond all statistics and stereotypes.

Beginning with the salt industry of the Kanawha Valley, the extraction of natural resources has evolved into the lifeblood of the economy. Today, West Virginia has become synonymous with coal

---

[4] Mari-Lynn Evans, Holly George-Warren, and Robert Santelli, *The Appalachians: America's First and Last Frontier* (New York: Random House, 2004), 7.
[5] E.g., "Proud wife/daughter/mother of a coal miner!"

mining.[6] Decades after the coal industry's heyday, state agencies still boast that West Virginia is the largest source of underground coal for the nation.[7] What's more, the relatively recent discovery of natural gas in the Marcellus and Utica Shales fosters hope that West Virginia's extraction economy can still thrive. Such hope belies the ignominy rooted in the state's lack of diversification. Bell and York claim the extraction industries have actively encouraged and exploited the state's proud coal-mining identity, with the effect that the population has unwittingly accepted the damage. They call this process "legitimation." Therefore, by industry design, West Virginians take great pride in the greatest cause of their dysfunction.[8]

But banking on natural resources has never really served West Virginia well. Some indeed have become very wealthy, but for many others, job loss, poverty, and poor educational attainment have followed the extraction industries from the start. Technological improvement has repeatedly put laborers out of work. Competition, environmental policies, and advances in alternative energy has caused unrecoverable economic spirals.[9] Unemployment and poverty has

---

[6] Thomas Shannon, "The Economy of Appalachia," in *A Handbook to Appalachia: An Introduction to the Region*, by Grace Toney. Edwards, JoAnn Aust Asbury, and Ricky L. Cox (Knoxville: University of Tennessee Press, 2006), 70.

[7] "West Virginia Coal Mining Facts," *Office of Miner's Health, Safety and Training*, accessed December 1, 2015. West Virginia may be the largest supplier of underground coal, but it is the second largest supplier of coal overall. Wyoming takes the top honor, though its coal comes primarily from strip mines. "U.S. Coal Production by State and by Rank" (Washington DC: National Mining Association, 2013), accessed December 1, 2015. See also Sue Greer-Pitt and David L. Rouse, "Natural Resources and Environment of Appalachia," in *A Handbook to Appalachia: An Introduction to the Region*, 59.

[8] Shannon Elizabeth Bell and Richard York, "Community Economic Identity: The Coal Industry and Ideology Construction in West Virginia," *Rural Sociology* 75, no. 1 (2010): 115-117, doi:10.1111/j.1549-0831.2009.00004.x.

[9] Bell and York demonstrate that industrial mechanization in timber and mining industries had already precipitated employment declines prior to the rise of environmental regulations, and they infer that more recent regulation is less to blame for unemployment than it is popular to believe ("Community Economic Identity," 113-114). In other words, unemployment has followed extraction

increased steadily in a state unprepared to explore opportunities unrelated to natural resources. Former congressman Alan Molohan has admitted that this lack of forward thinking has "left our communities ill-prepared for normal downturns in the business cycle—let alone by technological advances, increased overseas competition, and greater environmental sensitivities."[10]

In addition to unemployment and poverty, extraction industries have subjected the region to "a particular kind of economic development and its consequences," namely "unprecedented exploitation."[11] Glasmeier notes that "Central Appalachia, a region destroyed by rampant natural resource exploitation, remains mired in poverty because of complex historical circumstances that include a culture of exploitation, abuse and adaptive passivity."[12] These "places have been left behind...because capitalist development bankrupts localities socially, economically, politically, culturally, and environmentally."[13] The fact that massive amounts of land and natural resources are owned and controlled by private businesses outside the state continues to raise questions about whether the extraction

---

industries from their start.

[10] Mari-Lynn Evans, Holly George-Warren, and Robert Santelli, *Appalachians: America's First and Last Frontier* (New York: Random House, 2004), 153.

[11] Billings, "Culture and Poverty in Appalachia," 320-21. John Addison Teevan generalizes how undiversified extraction economies have historically resulted in population abuse and unhealthy societies: "The only way to accumulate wealth was to take it out of the ground. The accumulation of wealth in this kind of society created inequalities of income that were dramatically unjust. Wealthy people were generally selfish oppressors who got their wealth by taking it from ordinary people. That world grew very slowly, to one billion people around 1800, and was marked by servitude, slavery, famines, and a small elite of ruling wealth *extractors* who lived in luxury." John Addison Teevan, "Rawls and Economic Justice," in *John Rawls and Christian Social Engagement: Justice as Unfairness*, ed. Anthony B. Bradley and Greg Forster (Lexington: Lexington Books, 2014), 152.

[12] A.K. Glasmeier, "One Nation, Pulling Apart: The Basis of Persistent Poverty in the USA," *Progress in Human Geography* 26, no. 2 (2002): 170.

[13] A.K. Glasmeier, "One Nation, Pulling Apart," 156.

industries operate with West Virginia's best interests at heart.[14]

Reliance upon extraction industries has also contributed to the broader culture's devaluation of education, a problem that has consequences for Presbyterianism, which has historically thrived among more educated populations.[15] Simply put, coal mining never required advanced education, so the culture "eventually replaced the value of education with a strong work ethic, self-reliance, and commitment to family."[16] As commendable as these qualities are, what they have replaced has left the people less qualified for diversification and less compatible with Presbyterianism.

Less directly, but perhaps more systemically, the poverty that accompanies extraction industries has also devalued education. Sharon Teets summarizes how this happens:

> Although not unique to Appalachia, there is an integral linking of education and economics. Because resources have flowed from the region, and tax structures have not been altered significantly to tap into those resources, the mountainous regions of Appalachia, in particular, have suffered economically. The availability of funding for education and the jobs available for graduates of educational institutions are perhaps the two greatest factors in determining the quality of the education in the region.[17]

---

[14] "Who Owns West Virginia," *West Virginia Center on Budget and Policy*, 2013, accessed November 30, 2018, www.wvpolicy.org/land-study-paper-final3.pdf
[15] On the other hand, Wallace and Diekroger suggest it may also be "that the reverse is true: educational systems do not value or confirm the Appalachian culture." Lisa A. Wallace and Diane K. Diekroger, *'The ABCs in Appalachia': A Descriptive View of Perceptions of Higher Education in Appalachian Culture*, proceedings of Annual Conference of the Women of Appalachia: Their Heritage and Accomplishments, Zanesville, OH, October 26-28, 2000, 138.
[16] Wallace and Diekroger, *Perceptions of Higher Education in Appalachian Culture*, 138. This has changed over the years as mining has become more technical.
[17] Sharon Teet, "Education in Appalachia," in *A Handbook to Appalachia: An Introduction to the Region*, ed. Grace Toney Edwards, JoAnn Aust Asbury, and Ricky L. Cox (Knoxville: University of Tennessee Press, 2006), 35.

Centuries of such educational devaluation have led to devastating statistics. The Annie E. Casey Foundation ranks West Virginia among the worst states to educate children.[18] The percentage of the population holding a high school diploma is 47th in the nation.[19] The Appalachian Regional Commission reports that the "gap in college graduation rates between Appalachia and the rest of the nation" is widening, and "the lagging of central Appalachia, especially the distressed counties, is discouraging."[20] Correspondingly, West Virginia is consistently last in the percentage of the population with both undergraduate and graduate degrees.[21] The 2016 college-going rate for high school students in West Virginia was 55 percent, well under the national average of 69 percent.[22] Among the most recently calculated student cohort, only 30 percent of students graduated within four years—an improvement that is still well below the national average of 35 percent.[23] Far worse, the four-year graduation rate for at-risk students (an especially relevant statistic due to the prevalence of poverty) was only 21.5 percent.[24]

---

[18] "Education Rank in the United States," *Kids Count Data Center*, accessed March 27, 2019, datacenter.kidscount.org.

[19] "High School Diploma or Higher, by Percentage (Most Recent) by State," *Statemaster.com*, accessed March 27, 2019, www.statemaster.com. It should be noted that in recent years, graduation rates have been improving in spite of West Virginia's low ranking. According to the West Virginia Department of Education, as of 2018 the graduation rate is 90.2 %, third best in the nation (accessed March 28, 2019, zoomwv.k12.wv.us/Dashboard/portalHome.jsp).

[20] John Haaga, *Educational Attainment in Appalachia* (Washington, DC: Appalachian Regional Commission, 2004), 19. The distressed counties of central Appalachia overlap significantly with West Virginia.

[21] "Educational Attainment in West Virginia," *Statistical Atlas*, accessed March 28, 2019, www.statisticalatlas.com.

[22] *West Virginia Higher Education Report Card 2017* (Charleston WV: West Virginia Higher Education Policy Commission and Community and Technical College System of West Virginia, 2018), 3, accessed March 27, 2019, wvhepcdoc.wvnet.edu.

[23] *West Virginia Higher Education Report Card 2017*, 30.

[24] *West Virginia Higher Education Report Card 2017*, 31.

Unfortunately, the generational chain of poverty makes these statistics difficult to address in any systemic way. Richard Reeves of the Brookings Institute says that "poverty is 'sticky' across generations, especially for those born into deep poverty."[25] Federal and state policies have been implemented to improve educational access, methods, and resources over the years, but they have not commensurately improved West Virginia's educational rankings.[26] Even regional economic improvements are no guarantee that the outlooks, characteristics, and practices that originated in poverty will desist.[27] Recent upturns in the state's natural-resource-based economy threaten to sink the state deeper into its co-dependency with what may be most responsible for its current condition. In other words, West Virginia risks doubling down on a bad hand.

Higher education is certainly not the only solution to a lack of job diversification, but the situation as it is makes West Virginia less attractive to Presbyterianism (to its shame) and Presbyterianism less attractive to the population. Few places in West Virginia match up to the expectations of trendy suburban church planters. Demographers tout this place or that as "one of the fastest growing areas in the nation," none of which are in West Virginia. Thus, church planting agencies overlook West Virginia as a mission field, favoring locations with higher incomes, education,

---

[25] Emily Cuddy, Joanna Venator, and Richard V. Reeves, "In a Land of Dollars: Deep Poverty and Its Consequences," Brookings.edu, May 7, 2015, accessed December 12, 2015, www.brookings.edu/blogs.

[26] Teet overviews the history of government programs and policies in Appalachia with special attention to patterns and issues that "will likely continue to affect education in the region" ("Education in Appalachia," *A Handbook to Appalachia: An Introduction to the Region*, by Grace Toney. Edwards, JoAnn Aust Asbury, and Ricky L. Cox (Knoxville: University of Tennessee Press, 2006), 132-33).

[27] Ruby K. Payne in *Bridges Out of Poverty: Strategies for Professionals and Communities* (Highlands TX: Aha! Process, 2006) says, "An individual brings with him/her the hidden rules of the class in which he/she was raised. Even though the income of the individual may rise significantly, many patterns of thought, social interaction, cognitive strategies, etc., remain with the individual (7).

and upward mobility. As for evidence of Presbyterianism's unattractiveness to the population in general, one need only look at the relative success of "the competition," e.g., the Baptists and the Methodists.

West Virginia's condition also hinders the ability of existing churches to supply pulpits. Long-established churches find it difficult to bring in outside ministers because widespread financial distress limits what they can pay. Only those willing to work bi-vocationally can consider certain calls, a strongly negative prospect for outside recruits.[28] Low educational attainment, poverty, and geographic immobility also make it difficult for churches to locate, recruit, and educate ministerial candidates from within the state.

The State of Religion in West Virginia

West Virginia is like most other states with regard to religion. Nominal Christianity is on the decline. Mainline churches are struggling. Congregations, both mainline and evangelical, are generally small. The occasional "megachurch" has popped up in urban areas. The state has its fair share of both religious and non-religious people. Among the religious, it is as diverse as any other state.

---

[28] A 2004 Pulpit and Pew Research Report says, "The available evidence suggests that the congregations that are most vulnerable to pastoral vacancies are the smaller or rural ones, because these congregations have the fewest financial resources. . . . Rural congregations are also more isolated and have fewer job opportunities for spouses who might otherwise be able to supplement the pastor's salary and benefits. . . . The economic needs of full-time clergy and the limited resources of most small congregations make it difficult for these congregations to attract and retain qualified clergy." Patricia M. Y. Chang, *Assessing the Clergy Supply in the 21st Century* (Durham NC: Duke Divinity School, 2004), 12, accessed November 20, 2014, www.pulpitandpew.org. Another Pulpit and Pew Research Report notes that "Churches located in rural communities and economically depressed urban areas with intense pastoral and missional needs have little economic power and are therefore less appealing appointments and tend to have a rapid turnover of pastoral leadership." Becky R. McMillan and Matthew J. Price, *How Much Should We Pay the Pastor: A Fresh Look at Clergy Salaries for the 21st Century* (Durham NC: Duke Divinity School, 2003), 25, accessed November 20, 2014, www.pulpitandpew.org..

But West Virginia also has religious distinctives that are unique to (or at least greatly concentrated within) Appalachia.[29] Deborah Vansau McCauley labels these distinctives "Appalachian mountain religion." Among them are "pietism," "plain-folk camp-meeting religion," "revivalism and sacramentalism," and "the Separate Baptist religious culture of the early nineteenth century."[30] They reflect influences passed down from frontier beginnings, when Scotch-Irish heritage coalesced with the revivals of the Great Awakening to encourage "powerful expressions of emotional piety" that focused on the practical and personal experience of religion.[31] McCauley states, "Appalachian mountain religion as a regional religious tradition is the only venue in the United States in which the religiosity of the Scots-Irish first characterized by the Great Awakening of the Middle Colonies continues to flourish."[32]

Though Appalachian mountain religion has evolved, McCauley says that it still bears the imprint of the early Presbyterians: "Nearly all of the most celebrated camp meetings marking the height of the Great

---

[29] Melinda Bollar Wagner, "Religion in Appalachia," *A Handbook to Appalachia: An Introduction to the Region*, by Grace Toney Edwards, JoAnn Aust Asbury, and Ricky L. Cox (Knoxville: University of Tennessee Press, 2006), 182.

[30] A summary by Charles H. Lippy, "Appalachian Mountain Religion: A History (Book Review)," *Journal for the Scientific Study of Religion* 35, no. 1 (March 1996): 78.

[31] Deborah Vansau McCauley, *Appalachian Mountain Religion: A History* (Urbana: University of Illinois Press, 1995), 173. I found McCauley's book to be helpful, but she is not without her critics. One says that her work has been "muddied" by inferior research methodologies, researcher paternalism and bias, and a lack of primary source materials other than oral tradition (Jurretta Jordan Heckscher, review of *Appalachian Mountain Religion*, *American Studies International* 38, no. 3 (October 2000): 124). Donald Mathews of UNC Chapel Hill is critical of the label "Appalachian Mountain Religion," arguing that her bias has caused her to exclude denominational churches from the definition, even though specific denominational organizations are widely represented in the region ("Appalachian Mountain Religion (Book Review)," *Church History* 65 (December 1996): 773-774). See also James O. Farmer, "Appalachian Mountain Religion (Book Review)," *American Historical Review* 101 (December 1996): 1613.

[32] McCauley, *Appalachian Mountain Religion*, 176.

Revival started as Presbyterian sacramental meetings."[33] Due to geographical isolation, the Lord's Supper was celebrated infrequently, but these intensely pietistic meetings lasted for days, with services beginning on Friday and continuing through Monday. These easily become interdenominational gatherings, welcoming all professors of faith and intermingling traditions that eventually diluted Presbyterian distinctives. As revivalism quickly spread to other denominations, "plain-folk camp meetings" became a part of the warp and weft of Appalachia's religious society.[34]

The *Zeitgeist* of the Appalachian frontier may have encouraged this ecumenism and the correlative growth of the Baptists and Methodists. The Great Awakening thrust the Enlightenment spear deeply into the heart of American religion, aiding the progress of the nation toward revolution and independence. Disestablishmentarianism took root and began to displace the idea of an Established Church. Presbyterianism was a unique, early manifestation of this trend, combining grassroots authority with vestigial institutionalism. But the Great Awakening also set the stage for less institutional denominations by effectively taking religion out of the hands of the established churches and giving it to the common people—a sort of "social upheaval" in the face of the "ruling class."[35] The social climax of the Revolutionary War stoked the fires of anti-establishment individualism and continued to empower more diverse forms of religious expression.

The Second Awakening continued the process by diffusing revivalistic pietism throughout the Church down to the cellular level, empowering religious adherents to think independently regardless of education and skill. Armed with now-highly-valued Common Sense,

---

[33] McCauley, *Appalachian Mountain Religion*, 192.
[34] McCauley, *Appalachian Mountain Religion*, 191.
[35] Wesley M. Gewehr, *The Great Awakening in Virginia, 1740-1790* (Gloucester, MA: Duke University Press, 1965), 106 and 134.

generally and relatively illiterate religious adherents prioritized soul over society, simplicity over complexity, private interpretation over long-standing tradition, diversity over unity, independence over connectionalism, and new theologies over old. In this soil, truly grassroots denominations took root and grew invasively. The failure of the more connectional churches to supply the needs of the frontier aided their spread. Presbyterian laypersons sometimes forsook their own long-standing heritage for traditions that had more ready pastoral supply. Proponents of revivalism sometimes defected to the Baptists and Methodists where they could freely practice their more experiential religion. Under these influences and more, Appalachia nurtured a variety of denominational traditions that were independent, congregational, simple, and deeply focused on religious experience.[36]

The State of Presbyterianism in West Virginia

So, even though the original Ulster Scots brought their Calvinism with them, Presbyterianism was still sparsely represented in West Virginia by the 1800s.[37] Historians Rice and Brown note that since "about half of the five hundred Presbyterian churches in the colonies in 1776 were in areas from which West Virginia settlers were drawn, the state might well have become predominantly Presbyterian." However, "in 1800 nearly all of [Presbyterianism's] twenty-two congregations were in the Eastern Panhandle, the Northern Panhandle, and the Greenbrier Valley.

---

[36] Once again, I am indebted here to Mark Noll's *The Civil War as a Theological Crisis* and Bradley J. Longfield's *Presbyterians and American Culture: A History*.
[37] Stevan R. Jackson, "Peoples of Appalachia: Cultural Diversity within the Mountain Region," in *A Handbook to Appalachia: An Introduction to the Region*, ed. Grace Toney Edwards, JoAnn Aust Asbury, and Ricky L. Cox (Knoxville: University of Tennessee Press, 2006), 35. University of North Carolina at Chapel Hill professor H. Tyler Blethen notes the apparent contradiction that Presbyterianism was not more successful given the religious commitments of early West Virginia Settlers in "The Scotch-Irish Heritage of Southern Appalachia," *Appalachia Inside Out*, ed. Robert J. Higgs, Ambrose N. Manning, and Jim Wayne Miller, vol. 1, *Conflict and Change* (Knoxville: University of Tennessee Press, 1995), 5.

Table 5 Comparison of Denominations: 1850 and 2010

Denomination	1850	2010	
	Congregations	Congregations	Members
Methodists	281	1,251	141,223
Baptists	115	849	149,288
Presbyterians	61	215	21,235

As late as 1830, ten large counties of northcentral West Virginia, with a population of sixty thousand, had no settled Presbyterian minister with the exception of Asa Brooks, the pastor of the church at French Creek."[38] By 1838, the Greenbrier Presbytery had only fifteen churches between the Ohio River and the Allegheny Mountains.[39]

The plight of Presbyterianism appears even more dire when compared to the relative success of the two larger denominations at the time—by 1850 Presbyterians came in third to Baptists and Methodists by a wide margin. By 1860, Methodists and Baptists had eclipsed the Presbyterians by multiple thousands of members.[40] Over a hundred and fifty years later, the 2010 U.S. Religion Census shows that Presbyterianism has continued to be outpaced—the Methodists and Baptists have exceeded Presbyterian membership by better than 120,000 members each (Table 5).[41]

---

[38] Otis K Rice and Stephen W. Brown, *West Virginia: A History*, 65-66.
[39] *Lexington*, 101-02, 414-16.
[40] Rice and Brown, *West Virginia: A History*, 62. Joseph H. Dis DeBar, *The West Virginia Hand-Book and Immigrant's Guide: A Sketch of the State of West Virginia* (Parkersburg: Gibbons Bros, 1870), 167-68.
[41] Table 5 compares data from Rice and Brown (*West Virginia: A History*, 62) and the "2010 U.S. Religion Census: Religious Congregations & Membership Study" (Association of Religion Data Archives, *State Membership Report: West Virginia*, accessed November 19, 2014). However, the PC(USA)'s *Comparative Statistics 2012* lists approximately 5,000 fewer Presbyterians than the 2010 U.S. Religion Census. This number would not change significantly if all other Presbyterian denominations

As these denominations eclipsed Presbyterianism, Calvinist theology lost its inherited pride of place. Today, few West Virginians know what Calvinism is, and fewer still embrace it. Those who do know it typically believe it to be heterodox at best; others oppose it vehemently. To put it facetiously, mountaineers take their state motto very seriously, even regarding religion—for some, *Montani Semper Liberi* may as well translate as "Mountaineers have free will" or perhaps even "Mind your own religion." So, while "the Calvinism of Scots-Irish migrants...fused its own understanding of revivalism and sacramentalism" into Appalachian mountain religion (per McCauley), its doctrinal influence still declined.[42] The blame for this can be focused on two distinctives that proved to be Presbyterianism's greatest disadvantages: Connectionalism and the Educated Pulpit.

The Disadvantage of a Connectional Church

The Appalachian frontier was geographically disconnected and therefore a difficult place for a connectional church to thrive. A

---

in West Virginia were included, but they still underscore that the decline of Presbyterianism has been disproportionately negative. Presbyterian Mission Agency, *Comparative Statistics 2012: Information About Membership, Ministers, and Finances of the Presbyterian Church (USA)*, report, 2013, 3, accessed December 1, 2015.
[42] Lippy, "Appalachian Mountain Religion: A History (Book Review)," *Journal for the Scientific Study of Religion*, 78. Scots-Irish Calvinism may have disappeared, but it has been suggested that vestiges of it may remain in an endemic regional fatalism (Wagner, "Religion in Appalachia," 185-187). In the 1960's, Jack Weller famously diagnosed Appalachian fatalism in his much-debated book *Yesterday's People: Life in Contemporary Appalachia* (37-40); he also describes its impact on religion (128-133). It may exist in plain folk songs and choruses that contain "This World is Not My Home" theology (Dickson D. Bruce, *And They All Sang Hallelujah: Plain-folk Camp-meeting Religion, 1800-1845* (Knoxville: University of Tennessee Press, 1974)). Though as an Appalachian insider, I do not personally see this "Calvinistic Fatalism," I have gathered that it refers to sentiments like, "Life is hard; we cannot do anything about it; deal with it the best you can and move on." I personally question whether fatalism is indeed a defining characteristic of Appalachian culture or religion or the degree to which a Calvinist heritage is responsible for making it so. What some call fatalism may simply be the most realistic response to a hard life, which is certainly not exclusive to Appalachia.

simple fact of the frontier was that settlements were often isolated from one another, as were the churches within those settlements. This proved an obstacle for Presbyterian churches that, by definition, must connect with other churches. Elders from these churches met regularly to conduct business, but isolation made this difficult, and presbyteries struggled to recruit ministers who were willing to uproot their lives and settle into such deeply isolated communities. The few ministers who were already on the field travelled to meetings by horse for countless miles and were away from their parishes for days or weeks at time. This inconvenience instigated the creation of new presbyteries, as was the case when Lexington Presbytery spawned the Greenbrier in 1838. Even still, the Greenbrier covered the entire middle territory of West Virginia for well over fifty years, all the way from the Alleghenies to the Ohio River.

Pastor John McElhenney, perhaps the greatest presbyterian missionary in the state's history, grossly underestimated the size of this territory when he described it as "not less than one hundred and fifty miles square." But he summed up the problem accurately when he said,

> Presbyterianism has labored under peculiar disadvantages. . . . To reach these sparse settlements requires much laborious travelling on horseback; so that the itinerant system is much better adapted to a large portion of this region than the Presbyterian plan of settled pastors.[43]

When he began his six-decade ministry in 1808, he came into three pulpits that had already been without regular supply for years at a time. Churches like these tended to lose members to other traditions in which pastoral care was more readily available. As Banks well said, "Heritage was one thing, availability was something else."[44]

---

[43] *Recollections*, 260.
[44] Banks, *200 Years*, 38.

But Presbyterianism was not only crippled by geographic isolation. Survival in the hills and hollers encouraged cultural traits that did not mesh well with connectionalism. The Appalachian people have been described as fiercely independent,[45] and they may have viewed Presbyterianism's "highly centralized polity" suspiciously.[46] As the Scots-Irish settled the western waters, the "isolation and the exigencies of prolonged frontier life eroded old denominational ties" and left in their place an unattached religion with individualistic, congregational, and less institutional characteristics.[47]

Appalachians may have been known for their individualism (hence the state motto), but this did not exist outside a strong, collective, Appalachian identity.[48] Adherents of mountain religion shared a common identity of independence and self-reliance. Disconnected people struggling to survive in the hills found comfort in fellowship with those who suffered with them. Thus, this "collective individualism" was the perfect seed ground for a congregational religion that highly valued personal religious experience—they were each alone, yet all together. To these, Presbyterianism's more centralized and connected structure did not have the same appeal or adaptability as its competitors.

---

[45] On Appalachian individualism as a distinguishing characteristic, see the following: Wagner, "Religion in Appalachia," 188; Loyal Jones and Warren E. Brunner, *Appalachian Values* (Ashland, KY: Jesse Stuart Foundation, 1994), 52; Weller, *Yesterday's People,* 125-126.

[46] McCauley, *Appalachian Mountain Religion,* 436. See also F. Carlene Bryant: "The intimate relationship between individuals and their personal Savior admits very little in the way of centralized church authority and formal leadership" (*We're All Kin: A Cultural Study of a Mountain Neighborhood* (Knoxville: University of Tennessee, 1981), 97).

[47] Rice and Brown, *West Virginia: A History,* 62. Also, Jones and Brunner: "For a people escaping the infringements of church and state, Appalachia was ideal for a new way of life, for a time, away from 'powers and principalities.'" *Appalachian Values,* 24.

[48] Wagner, "Religion in Appalachia," 188-89.

On the other hand, the Baptists and Methodists thrived with a "structure and philosophy" better suited to the frontier. Baptists benefited from an independent, congregational democracy, and the Methodists benefited from a flexible organizational structure that was "ideally suited to the conditions in West Virginia."[49] Methodists were also connectional, but utilizing lay leaders and circuit riders, they were better able to establish and maintain an enduring and ubiquitous presence that, along with the Baptists, appealed to a "strong grassroots base."[50]

The oxymorons of independent congregationalism and collective individualism are still a problem for presbyterian connectionalism today. Of course, these are generalizations (though hopefully not stereotypes), and exceptions will always exist. But it seems true to experience that West Virginia churches highly value both independence and congregational polity. Today, this experience is borne out every time West Virginia Presbyterians see congregationalism peeking its head up from behind their own church pews.

The Disadvantage of a Learned Ministry

Since its origins, Presbyterianism has always expected its ministers to be well-trained and highly educated. Educational qualifications were

---

[49] Rice and Brown, *West Virginia: A History*, 63. Gewehr extensively contrasts advantages and disadvantages of the organizational structure of Baptists, Methodists, and Presbyterians and shows how these relate to their relative success (or lack thereof) in pioneering and colonial America (195-198). He credits Baptist success to its anti-Established-Church appeal; to the appeal of an uneducated, non-exclusive clergy to "unlettered men;" and to the rise of libertarianism in colonial America, among other reasons (134-135). Although early Methodism was a part of the Established Church, Gewehr say that its success can be credited to six compensatory advantages: 1) itinerant ministries, 2) reliance upon lay ministers, 3) local organization, 4) established hymnody, 5) broadly appealing theology, and 6) the printing and distribution of religious literature (162-165). He adds that it was a "strong popular movement" and that its status in the Established Church allowed it to operate unpersecuted by the Anglicans (166).

[50] Rice and Brown, *West Virginia: A History*, 63. Cf. Gewehr, *The Great Awakening in Virginia*, 166.

even an issue (one of several) that divided the church for a time during the Old-Side New Side Controversy of the eighteenth century.[51] When ministers who met these educational standards were unavailable, frontier communities "had to do what they had to do" to receive pastoral care. In some cases, this meant supporting other denominations.

On top of Appalachia's normal geographic exigencies, both the Great Awakenings and the expanding frontier greatly increased the demand for ministers. While Presbyterianism begrudgingly benefited from the Awakening, it simply was not as capable of riding the wave as easily as other traditions. Extensive ordination requirements (e.g. education, training, probation, examination, etc.) created a severe ministerial shortfall. According to Presbyterian tradition, even congregations-already-in-place, though ready and willing, could only be organized as churches by ordained ministers. But candidates sometimes continued in the ordination process for years before finally qualifying to organize churches. As a result, other denominations and religious traditions stepped in to fill the void, establishing themselves as the default religious presence throughout the western waters. Even when seminaries evolved to "mass produce" ministers, Presbyterians still could not supply enough pastors to organize churches and fill pulpits.[52] On the other hand, Baptist and Methodist traditions could do so easily enough to saturate the culture and supplant Presbyterianism.

But the disadvantages of the learned ministry were not just geographic and circumstantial—they were also cultural. In mountain religion, "a direct experience of God's power was felt to be far superior to any enlightenment that might be gained from a worldly education."[53]

---

[51] *Kanawha*, 32-38.
[52] A "shortage of Presbyterian seminaries in the eighteenth century made it difficult for Scotch-Irish frontier communities to find qualified clergymen to minister to their needs" (Blethen, "The Scotch-Irish Heritage of Southern Appalachia," 6).
[53] Bryant, *We're All Kin*, 98.

Thus, the educated pulpit placed a social and theological wedge between Presbyterianism and a culture that valued simple, pietistic religion: "The Presbyterian emphasis on intellectualization, its demand for a learned ministry, and its lack of emotional appeal were deadly to mountain people."[54] Other denominations, on the other hand, benefited from "a decided tendency to underrate education… [Their] lack of education was a decided advantage…for it placed them on the same plane with those to whom they ministered, and a strong bond of sympathy developed between the two."[55] Presbyterianism "'with its intellectual demands of an elaborate creed'…was never able to reach and to stir the common folk as the Baptists did."[56] It "appealed more to the cultured and educated and less to the common people which made it easier for the developing Methodists and Baptists to make inroads into Presbyterian communities. The ministers read their long sermons which were scholarly discourses, often unrelated to the life and needs of the people."[57] Conversely, Methodist and Baptist preaching was "much more easily comprehended than was Calvinism and had the advantage of placing everyone on an exactly equal plane in the sight of God."[58]

Woodworth in his *History of the Presbytery of Winchester* explained the presbyterian problem as he observed it in the Valley of Virginia, a territory which overlapped West Virginia's Eastern Panhandle and faced similar difficulties:

> In the realm of money Gresham's Law applies, to wit that when two currencies circulate in exchange on a parity basis, the coinage of lesser intrinsic worth drives the coinage of greater intrinsic worth out of circulation. That law applies also in religion. . .. A purer faith with high

---

[54] McCauley, *Appalachian Mountain Religion,* 436. Cf. Bryant, *We're All Kin,* 98-99.
[55] Gewehr, *The Great Awakening in Virginia,* 113.
[56] *Lexington,* 106.
[57] *Lexington,* 107.
[58] Gewehr, *The Great Awakening in Virginia,* 165.

moral ideals gives way to easier ways to serve God. Methodism and Baptistism, with lower standards of ministerial education and laxer ideals as to discipline and the support of the religion, drove both the Episcopal and the Presbyterian Churches out of the Northern Neck below Fredericksburg. In the words of Bishop Meade: "The whole population was incorporated in other denominations;" because of their easier ways to serve God. That law applies to the disappearance of the Presbyterian congregations elsewhere. . .. Perhaps matters might have turned out better if the Presbyterians had used their lay eldership in the Methodist way as local preachers and class leaders. [59]

A bit closer to home, the testimony of the Reverend Henry Ruffner illustrates how both connectionalism and the educated pulpit hindered his own ministry. While he preached to the *Society of Christians Called Presbyterians* in the Kanawha Valley during his probation and prior to his ordination (1815 to 1819), he was also regularly preaching to Christians in two other locations around Kanawha—in Pocatalico to the north and in Teays Valley to the west. Of his ministry in Pocatalico he wrote,

Most of my labors outside of Charleston and the Saltworks, were directed towards the parts of the country where the people had little or no preaching of any kind and where no Christian Society existed. I preached on Elk river as far up as the settlements then extended. I was the first minister who ever preached in the upper settlements of Pocatalico; and could, a year after I began to visit that people, have organized a Presbyterian Church there; but being as yet a mere licentiate, I could not regularly organize a church. Before I was ordained, and had authority to organize a church, a Methodist brother, who towards the last, began to join me in my visits to that region, succeeded in organizing a Methodist Society there. Having enough to do elsewhere, I then gave up that new ground to my Methodist brethren, and was pleased to hear that they continued to cultivate with

---

[59] *Winchester*, 12-13.

success a field in which I had first and not a few times preached the gospel. But whilst I rejoiced that others had successfully entered upon a field which I had labored to prepare, I was then and am to this day convinced that our Presbyterian system is defective in its ways and means of providing for the spiritual wants of a new country, such as Kanawha then was.

And of his work in Teays Valley he wrote,

The other church was in Teaze's Valley about 18 miles from Charleston. Its members were nearly as numerous as those of the other church. This might have grown to be a strong church, had it been attended to by my successors in Kanawha. But having been neglected for years its members gave up in despair and joined other denominations.[60]

As more successful ecclesial traditions settled deeper into popular religious culture, Presbyterianism's peculiarities faced the corollary disadvantage of theological prejudice, a problem described by McElhenny at the inauguration of the Greenbrier Presbytery 1838:

Not only will we have to contend with the pride of the natural heart, and the opposition to the gospel, which are characteristics of fallen man, but, in some places, with no small amount of prejudice against Presbyterianism. Not a few view it as a system of fatalism, alike derogatory to the character of God, and subversive of man's accountability; or they have been taught to consider it as only another name for infidelity. But, however strong these prejudices may be, I have never yet known them to have so firm a hold upon the mind that they will not, in a great measure, if not entirely, give way when the doctrines which are taught in the Confession of Faith, which we believe, and which we preach, are plainly presented to any people. They are very different from the caricatures of Presbyterianism which are too often exhibited by those who differ with us in doctrine.

---

[60] "Henry Ruffner, West Virginia Historical Magazine Quarterly, April 1902," *West Virginia Archives and History*, accessed March 21, 2019, www.wvculture.org.

This prejudice surfaced early, as Henry Ruffner humorously showed in the *Southern Literary Messenger* of 1856. He told the story (the truth of which he took special pains to affirm) of the Reverend "Little Billy" Willson, who in the early 1800s traveled through the Kanawha Valley on his way to Kentucky. There he encountered "Old Billy" Morris, a prominent community leader and family patriarch:

> [Old Billy Morris] was wholly illiterate. He could neither read nor write— at least not so as to profit by these acquirements....It may be readily supposed that such a man was bigoted in his opinions, and full of prejudices. Strong-minded, self-relying men, not liberalized by education, always are. He was not disposed to tolerate opposition to his will, neither would he regard those with favor who differed from him in religion or politics. He was a Baptist, wholly and exclusively. He knew little of other religious denominations, and had imbibed unfavorable opinions of them. He seems to have somehow gotten a particular dislike to the Presbyterians, which was rather unfortunate at first for our Little Bobby Willson . . . .

> It being Saturday evening when he arrived, Mr. Willson was properly concerned to discover how he might spend the next day in a Christian manner, and whether, providentially, a way might be opened for him to do a little good among these heathenish, whiskey-drinking, bear-hunting barbarians of Kanawha; —for such was the character which he had heard of them.

> When little Bobby saw what a corpulent backwoodsman he had for his host, —how loudly and authoritatively he spoke to those around him— how rough were his manners, and how dogmatical his conversation, he was almost afraid to say a word to him about religious worship.

> But in the course of the evening, he found that Mr. Morris was, himself, a member of the Baptist church, and that his rudeness of manner proceeded not from ungodliness, but from early association with rude and ignorant backwoodsmen. Therefore, he ventured, before going to bed, to inquire if there was to be any preaching in the neighborhood on the morrow. "No," said his host. "None higher than Elk [River]."

174

"How far is that Mr. Morris?"

"Eighteen miles."

"Well, Mr. Morris, as I am a preacher of the gospel, and do not wish to travel, or to be idle, on the Sabbath, would it be convenient and agreeable to have preaching appointed for me in this neighborhood? I suppose that a small congregation could be collected."

"What profession are you of?"

"I am a Presbyterian."

"A Presbyterian are you! Then you can't preach about here. We are all Baptists, and have not much opinion about your sort o' people."[61]

Continuing Problems for the Continuing Church

No matter the difficulties, Presbyterians continued organizing churches, starting schools, and working to improve communities throughout the nineteenth and twentieth centuries. Between 1800 and the Civil War, around seventy new churches were organized. After the Civil War until the turn of the century, around 112 churches were started. In the first four decades of the twentieth century, an additional 130 came to be. By the time the comprehensive *Inventory of the Church Archives of West Virginia: The Presbyterian Churches* was compiled in 1941, nearly 320 Presbyterian churches had existed at one time or another in West Virginia territory.

Unfortunately for Presbyterianism in the Great State of West Virginia, the influx of Modernism in the 1920s began diminishing the evangelical fervor that had once characterized previous generations. In *Christianity in Appalachia*, Yeuell and Meyers describe this downturn as

---

[61] "Kanawha Pieces," *Southern Literary Messenger* 22, no. 5, (May 1856): 359-363. The story continues on an ironic note: Rev. Willson traveled to the Elk River the next morning, where he received a warm reception by the Baptist congregation that met in the woods. There he preached and was begged to stay and preach a few more days before moving on to Kentucky.

two interrelated phenomena. The first was that the "protestant evangelical consensus gave way to religious pluralism," bringing about a "religious depression and spiritual lethargy." The second was that the "fundamentalist-modernist controversy...dissipated the church's energy for missions."[62] Thus, in contrast with its great history, mainline Presbyterianism gave up its place as a bastion for the Gospel, at least as the presbyterian pioneers once preached it.

As Modernism and progressivism continued conquering Presbyterianism over the course of the twentieth century, the mainline churches also abrogated their commitment to the inspiration and authority of the Bible, to the Westminster Standards, and to the need for and exclusivity of salvation through the Gospel. In the years following the collapse of their evangelical commitments, they continued diligently serving the temporal needs of the people of Appalachia, for which they are to be strongly commended. But lacking evangelistic impetus, Presbyterianism surrendered its spiritual mission. McElhenney's prescient words could just as well apply today:

> It is entirely a mistaken idea to suppose that truth and religion can be promoted by accommodating them to the prejudices of the world; and that minister of Jesus Christ who endeavors to do this, does just so much to destroy the truth of the Bible, and the saving influences of religion on the hearts of impenitent sinners. The question with us is not, What will suit the prejudices of the world; but, What does the Bible say? What has God revealed? And whatever these are, we must preach them, whether the world will hear or whether they will forbear. Nor have we the least evidence to believe that our preaching will be successful in any other way. God is truth; his word is truth; and nothing but truth will ever succeed in the salvation of sinners.

---

[62] H. Davis Yeuell and Marcia Clark Myers, "The Presbyterians in Central Appalachia," *Christianity in Appalachia*, ed. Bill J. Leonard (Knoxville: University of Tennessee Press, 1999), 194.

One hundred seventy years later, the occasional modern voice within Mainline Presbyterianism still echoes McElhenney's warning. The late Reverend Dr. John H. Leith was a professor at Virginia's historic Union Theological seminary and a prophetic voice to the mainline churches. He wrote the following in his book *The Reformed Imperative: What the Church Has to Say That No One Else Can Say*:

> The primary source of the malaise of the church, however, is the loss of a distinctive Christian message and of the theological and biblical competence that made its preaching effective. Sermons fail to mediate the presence and grace of God. Many sermons are moral exhortations, which can be heard delivered with greater skill at the Rotary or Kiwanis Club. Many sermons are political and economic judgments on society, which have been presented with greater wisdom and passion at political conventions. Many sermons offer personal therapies, which can be better provided by well-trained psychiatrists. The only skill the preacher has—or the church, for that matter—which is not found with greater excellence somewhere else, is theology, in particular the skill to interpret and apply the Word of God in sermon, teaching, and pastoral care. This is the great service which the minister and the church can render the world. Why should anyone come to church for what can be better found somewhere else?[63]

Meanwhile, the evangelical denominations are growing steadily in most parts of the nation. In West Virginia, however, they lack resources and face many of the same obstacles as the Presbyterians of old. Nevertheless, they faithfully preach the same gospel John McElhenney and Henry Ruffner preached two hundred years ago. But at the time of this writing, the *Presbyterian Church in America* has only ten churches. The *Evangelical Presbyterian Church* and the *Associate Reformed Presbyterian Church* each have only three. The

---

[63] John H. Leith, *The Reformed Imperative: What the Church Has to Say That No One Else Can Say* (Louisville KY: Westminster John Knox Press, 1988), 22.

Orthodox Presbyterian Church, the *Communion of Reformed Evangelical Churches*, and *ECO: A Covenant Order of Evangelical Presbyterians* each have two.[64]

Lest evangelical Presbyterianism's small footprint crush hopes and diminish prayers, it should be noted that these twenty-two churches are still more than the fifteen Greenbrier had at its inauguration and from which hundreds more eventually descended. May today's churches be as inspired as they were by what John McElhenney preached on that occasion:

> That the gospel may be preached to lost sinners, and that the great object of the ministry may be accomplished, each individual member, every church, minister, presbytery, synod, and General Assembly have their peculiar part to act. They have their field of operations, through which they must pass, and which they must cultivate, that it may bring forth fruit unto God. They stand as so many detached parties to prepare the way for the general spread of the gospel, and as instruments to bring about that day when it shall be preached to all nations, kindreds, and tongues, and peoples.
>
> We, as a presbytery, have had our field marked out. The Synod of Virginia has said to us, "You shall occupy a portion of this State which lies west of the Alleghany Mountains." And now it is not a matter of option with us whether we shall occupy it or not. It is not a matter of mere convenience with us, but a matter of sacred and solemn obligation. The duty which we owe God; the duty which we owe the church, ourselves, and others, imperiously demands that we should endeavor in the strength of our God to set up our banner here.

---

[64] Readers may locate these churches by their denominational websites: pcanet.org, opc.org, epc.org, crechurches.org, and arpchurch.org. ECO (eco-pres.org) is a recent division from the PC(USA), catalyzed by the PC(USA)'s theological modernism and progressive social positions, though it still downplays confessional subscription and encourages egalitarianism.

SELECTED BIBLIOGRAPHY

Presbytery Histories

Courtney, Lloyd McFarland. *The Church on the Western Waters: An History of Greenbrier Presbytery and Its Churches*. Richmond: Whittet & Shepperson, 1940.

Ellis, Dorsey D. *Look Unto the Rock: A History of the Presbyterian Church, in West Virginia from 1719 to 1974*. Parsons, WV: McClain Printing Company, 1982.[1]

Morton, John Blair, and Robert Kemp Morton, eds. *History of the Presbytery of Kanawha, 1895-1956*. Charleston, WV: Jarrett Print, 1957.

Slade, Andrew G., ed. *Presbyterianism in the Upper Ohio Valley: Bicentennial U.S.A. July 1976*. Steubenville, OH: Presbytery of the Upper Ohio Valley, 1976.

Wilson, Gill I. *The Story of Presbyterianism in West Virginia*. n.p., 1958.

Wilson, Howard McKnight. *The Lexington Presbytery Heritage: The Presbytery of Lexington and Its Churches in the Synod of Virginia Presbyterian Church in the United States, 1786-1970*. Verona, VA: McClure Press, 1971.

Woodworth, Robert Bell. *History of the Presbytery of Winchester (Synod of Virginia): Its Rise and Growth, Ecclesiastical Relations, Institutions and Agencies, Churches and Ministers 1719-1945*. Staunton, VA: McClure Printing, 1947.

Work Projects Administration. *Inventory of the Church Archives of West Virginia: The Presbyterian Churches*. Charleston, WV: West Virginia Historical Records Survey, 1941.

Histories of Appalachia and West Virginia

Drake, Richard B. *A History of Appalachia*. Lexington, KY: University Press of Kentucky, 2003.

Rice, Otis K. *The Allegheny Frontier: West Virginia Beginnings, 1730-1830*. Lexington: University Press of Kentucky, 1970.

---

[1] I did not become aware of this text until after I wrote this book and have only been able to reference it in footnotes.

Rice, Otis K. *West Virginia: The State and Its People*. Parsons, WV: McClain Printing Company, 1979.

Rice, Otis K., and Stephen W. Brown. *West Virginia: A History*. Lexington, KY: University Press of Kentucky, 1993.

Williams, John Alexander. *Appalachia: A History*. Chapel Hill NC: The University of North Carolina Press, 2002

Miscellaneous

Abney, Katie Bell. *History of the Presbyterian Congregation and the Other Early Churches of "Kenhawha" 1804-1900*. Charleston, WV: First Presbyterian Church, 1930.

Baldwin, Leland D. *The Keelboat Age on Western Waters*. Pittsburgh: University of Pittsburgh Press, 1980.

Banks, James W. *200 Years from Good Hope*. Parsons, WV: McClain Print., 1983.

Banks, Taunya Lovell. "Colorism: A Darker Shade of Pale." *UCLA Law Review*, 47 (2000): 1705-746.

Bell, Shannon Elizabeth and Richard York, "Community Economic Identity: The Coal Industry and Ideology Construction in West Virginia." *Rural Sociology* 75, no. 1 (2010): 115-117. doi:10.1111/j.1549-0831.2009.00004.x.

Billings, Dwight "Culture and Poverty in Appalachia: A Theoretical Discussion and Empirical Analysis." *Social Forces* 53, no. 2 (1974): 315-323.

Bills, Dennis E. *An Unobstructed Educational Model for Ministerial Candidates of the New River Presbytery of the Presbyterian Church in America*. Doctor of Ministry thesis, Pittsburgh Theological Seminary, 2016.

Bills, Dennis E. *A Church You Can See: Building a Case for Church Membership*. New Martinsville, WV: ReformingWV Publications, 2017.

Bradley, Anthony B. and Greg Forster, eds. *John Rawls and Christian Social Engagement: Justice as Unfairness*. Lexington: Lexington Books, 2014.

Brantly, J. E. *History of Oil Well Drilling*. Houston: Gulf Publ. Comp., 1971.

Brown, James Moore. *The Captives of Abb's Valley: A Legend of Frontier Life*. Philadelphia: Presbyterian Board of Publication and Sabbath-School Work, 1854.

Brown, James Moore. *The Captives of Abb's Valley: Revised and Annotated.* Dennis Eldon Bills, ed. New Martinsville WV: ReformingWV Publications, 2019.

Bryant, F. Carlene. *We're All Kin: A Cultural Study of a Mountain Neighborhood.* Knoxville: University of Tennessee, 1981.

Chang, Patricia M. Y. *Assessing the Clergy Supply in the 21st Century.* Durham NC: Duke Divinity School, 2004.

Coghill, Ruth P. *The First Presbyterian Church Charleston West Virginia: A Brief History.* n.p., n.d.

Coghill, Ruth Putney. *The Church of 150 Years.* Charleston, WV: First Presbyterian Church, 1969.

Coonts, Violet Gadd, Gilbert Gray Coonts, and Harold Gadd. *The Western Waters: Early Settlers of Eastern Barbour County, West Virginia.* Denver: Stephen P. Coonts, 1991.

Dickson, Bruce D. *And They All Sang Hallelujah: Plain-folk Camp-meeting Religion, 1800-1845.* Knoxville: University of Tennessee Press, 1974.

Diss DeBar, Joseph H. *The West Virginia Hand-Book and Immigrant's Guide: A Sketch of the State of West Virginia.* Parkersburg: Gibbons Bros, 1870

Dunaway, Wilma A. *The First American Frontier: Transition to Capitalism in Southern Appalachia, 1700-1860.* Chapel Hill: University of North Carolina Press, 1996.

Edwards, Grace Toney, JoAnn Aust Asbury, and Ricky L. Cox, eds. *A Handbook to Appalachia: An Introduction to the Region.* Knoxville: University of Tennessee Press, 2006.

Evans, Mari-Lynn, Holly George-Warren, and Robert Santelli, eds. *The Appalachians: America's First and Last Frontier.* New York: Random House, 2004.

Forman, Cyrus. *A Briny Crossroads: Salt, Slavery, and Sectionalism in the Kanawha Salines.* Master's thesis, City College of New York, 2014. Accessed July 2, 2018. https://academicworks.cuny.edu/cgi /viewcontent.cgi?article=1274&context=cc_etds_theses.

Fry, Rose W. *Recollections of the Rev. John McElhenney, D.D.* Richmond, VA: Whittet & Shepperson, Printers, 1893.

Gewehr, Wesley M. *The Great Awakening in Virginia, 1740-1790.* Gloucester, MA: Duke University Press, 1965.

Glasmeier, A. K. "One Nation, Pulling Apart: The Basis of Persistent Poverty in the USA." *Progress in Human Geography* 26, no. 2 (2002).

Graham, James R. *The Planting of the Presbyterian Church in Northern Virginia Prior to the Organization of Winchester Presbytery.* Winchester, VA: Geo. F. Norton Publishing, 1904.

Graham, Jr., Preston D. *A Kingdom Not of This World: Stuart Robinson's Struggle to Distinguish the Sacred from the Secular during the Civil War.* Macon GA: Mercer University Press, 2002.

Guthrie, Dwight R. *John McMillan, The Apostle of Presbyterianism in the West, 1752-1833.* Pittsburgh: University of Pittsburgh Press, 1952.

Harold, Stanley. *Border War: Fighting over Slavery before the Civil War.* Chapel Hill NC: The University of North Carolina Press, 2010.

Hart, D.G. and Mark Noll, eds. *Dictionary of the Presbyterian Reformed Tradition in America.* Downers Grove IL: InterVarsity Press, 1999.

Higgs, Robert J., Ambrose N. Manning, and Jim Wayne Miller. *Appalachia Inside Out.* Knoxville: University of Tennessee Press, 1995.

Historical and Biographical Catalog of the Officers and Students of the Western Theological Seminary of the Presbyterian Church at Allegheny City, Penn'a, 1827-1885. Allegheny PA: Published by the Seminary, 1885.

Hodge, Charles. *What Is Presbyterianism.* Philadelphia: Presbyterian Board of Education, 1855.

Jones, Loyal and Warren E. Brunner. *Appalachian Values.* Ashland, KY: Jesse Stuart Foundation, 1994.

Kelso, Brian. "Credentialing for the Gospel Ministry in the PCA." White paper, Lamp Theological Seminary, n.d. Accessed March 29, 2019. http://lampseminary.org/wp-content/uploads/2015/10/Credentialing-for-the-Gospel-Ministry-in-the-PCA.pdf

Laidley, W. S., ed. *The West Virginia Historical Magazine Quarterly, Volumes 3-5.* Charleston, WV: West Virginia Historical and Antiquarian Society, 1903. Accessed May 30, 2018. https://books.google.com/books?id=6_QxAQAAMAAJ&dq=.

Leith, John H. *The Reformed Imperative: What the Church Has to Say That No One Else Can Say.* Louisville KY: Westminster John Knox Press, 1988.

Lincoln University College and Theological Seminary Biographical Catalog. Lancaster PA: Press of the New Era, 1918.

Lloyd, James T. *Lloyd's Steamboat Directory and Disasters on the Western Waters.* Chicago: D.B. Cooke and Co., 1856.

Longfield, Bradley. *Presbyterians and American Culture: A History.* Louisville KY: Westminster John Knox Press, 2013.

Loomis, Elisha Scott. *Descendants of Joseph Loomis in America: And His Antecedents in the Old World.* Self-published, 1909.

Lucas, Sean Michael. *For a Continuing Church: The Roots of the Presbyterian Church in America.* Phillipsburg NJ: P&R Publishing Company, 2015.

McCauley, Deborah Vansau . *Appalachian Mountain Religion: A History.* Urbana: University of Illinois Press, 1995).

McDaniel, John M., Charles N. Watson, and David T. Moore. *Liberty Hall Academy: The Early History of the Institutions Which Evolved into Washington and Lee University.* Lexington VA: Liberty Hall Press, 1979.

McLeod, Alexander. *Negro Slavery Unjustifiable: A Discourse.* New York: T. & F. Swords, 1802.

McMillan, Becky R. and Matthew J. Price. *How Much Should We Pay the Pastor: A Fresh Look at Clergy Salaries for the 21st Century.* Durham NC: Duke Divinity School, 2003.

Montgomery, John Fleshman. *History of the Old Stone Presbyterian Church 1783-1983.* Parsons, WV: McClain Printing Company, 1983.

Noll, Mark. *The Civil War as a Theological Crisis.* Chapel Hill, NC: The University of North Carolina Press, 2006.

Payne Ruby K. *Bridges Out of Poverty: Strategies for Professionals and Communities.* Highlands TX: Aha! Process, 2006.

Plan of the Western Theological Seminary of the Presbyterian Church in the United States of America: Founded 1825. Allegheny PA: J.H. McFarland, 1884.

Price, William T. *Historical Sketch of Greenbrier Presbytery.* Lewisburg, WV: Greenbrier Independent Print., 1889.

Robinson, Stuart. *Discourses of Redemption as Revealed in Sundry Times and Diverse Manners.* Richmond VA: Presbyterian Committee of Publication, 1866.

Robinson, Stuart. *Slavery as Recognized in the Mosaic Civil Law, Recognized Also, and Allowed, in the Abrahamic, Mosaic, and Christian Church.* Toronto: Rollo & Adam, 1865.

Rowe, Larry L. *Booker T. Washington: Pre-Civil War History of Slavery, Salt and his Boyhood Home in Malden West Virginia.* Charleston WV: West Virginia State University Press, 2019.

Rowe, Larry L. *History Tour of Old Malden Virginia and West Virginia: Booker T. Washington's Formative Years.* Self-published, 2014.

Ruffner, Henry. "Kanawha Pieces," *Southern Literary Messenger* 22, no. 5, (May 1856): 359-363.

Ruffner, Henry. *Address to the People of West Virginia.* Lexington VA: L. C. Noel, 1847.

Ruffner, Henry. *Union Speech; Delivered at Kanawha Salines, Va., on the Fourth of July, 1856.* Cincinnati OH: Applegate and Co., 1856.

Samples, Lori, transcriber. *160th Anniversary of Greenbrier County Commemorative Booklet.* Accessed December 16, 2018. www.wvgenweb.org/greenbrier/history/160th10.html.

Scott, E.C., comp. *Ministerial Directory of the Presbyterian Church, U.S. 1861-1941.* Austin TX: Press of Von Boeckmann-Jones Co., 1942.

Stec, Stephen. "Catarina Beierlin's Gravestone Revisited." *The Magazine of the Jefferson County Historical Society* 82 (December 2016): 17-32.

Sullivan, Ken, ed. *The West Virginia Encyclopedia.* Charleston WV: The West Virginia Humanities Council, 2006.

Thompson, Earnest Trice. *Presbyterians in the South: Volume One: 1607-1861.* Richmond VA: John Knox Press, 1963.

Thompson, Earnest Trice. *Presbyterians in the South: Volume Two: 1861-1890.* Richmond VA: John Knox Press, 1973.

Wallace, Lisa A. and Diane K. Diekroger. 'The ABCs in Appalachia': A *Descriptive View of Perceptions of Higher Education in Appalachian Culture.* Proceedings of Annual Conference of the Women of Appalachia: Their Heritage and Accomplishments. Zanesville, OH, October 26-28, 2000.

Washington, Booker T. *Up from Slavery.* Garden City, NY: Doubleday and Company, 1901.

Weller, Jack. *Yesterday's People: Life in Contemporary Appalachia.* Lexington KY: University of Kentucky Press, 1965.

APPENDICES

APPENDIX A

A Sermon Delivered at the First Meeting of the Greenbrier Presbytery[1]

"In the name of our God we will set up our banners."
— Psalm: xx., middle clause of the 5th verse.

Introduction

This psalm was written immediately before David engaged in conflict with the Ammonites and Syrians. It is the prayer of Israel for the success of their king in this perilous undertaking.

No words could be better suited to our particular situation than these. True, we are not about to engage in a perilous conflict. But we have been recently formed into a presbytery. Our field of labor has been assigned us — a field not only large, but one that presents more than ordinary difficulties. But if we can, from the heart, adopt the spirit of this psalm; if we do indeed feel that our strength is alone in God; if we go forth under his special direction and protection, then may we be assured, that "in the name of our God we will set up our banners."

In the further treatment of these words I shall pursue the following order:

I. Notice some of the difficulties with which we will have to contend in setting up our banners in this region of country.

II. The means which, under God, we must use to accomplish this end.

---

[1] One of two sermons edited for print by John McElhenney and reproduced as Appendices in *Recollections*. He preached this one in 1838 at the inauguration of the Greenbrier Presbytery. The second was at his semicentenary celebration in Lewisburg in 1858. The headings and subheadings are my own.

III. By way of appendix, give you a concise view of the rise of Presbyterianism in this region which we propose to occupy.

Before I proceed to these points I shall say a word by way of explanation.

To set up a banner, flag, or ensign, generally implies that possession is taken of that country, town, or city where this is done, and that they are brought under subjection to another power. This is the sense in which the word is used in the text. But we wish it understood that, so far as other Christian denominations are concerned, this is not the sense in which we use the term; that we do not present ourselves in the character of Presbyterians, supposing that, as a matter of right, we are to occupy this extensive region to the exclusion of all others. No, we assume no such prerogative. We love our own church. We prefer it to every other. We believe that in doctrine and order it is nearer to the apostolic model than any other portion of the visible church. But we do not believe that the visible church is confined to the limits of our denomination, and that we alone have authority from the Head of the church to preach the gospel and administer the ordinances. Nor would we place even the least obstacle in the way of others. We would most cordially take them by the hand and say, We bid you Godspeed in the common cause.

Our Sacred and Solemn Obligation

But to return to the first point deduced from the text, which was to notice some of the difficulties with which we will have to contend in setting up our banner in this region of country;

That the gospel may be preached to lost sinners, and that the great object of the ministry may be accomplished, each individual member, every church, minister, presbytery, synod, and General Assembly have their peculiar part to act. They have their field of operations, through which they must pass, and which they must cultivate, that it may bring forth fruit unto God. They stand as so many detached parties to prepare the way for the general spread of the gospel, and as instruments to bring about that day when it shall be preached to all nations, kindreds, and tongues, and peoples.

We, as a presbytery, have had our field marked out. The Synod of Virginia has said to us, You shall occupy a portion of this State which lies west of the Alleghany Mountains. And now it is not a matter of option with us whether we shall occupy it or not. It is not a matter of mere convenience with us, but a matter of sacred and solemn obligation. The duty which we owe God; the duty which we owe the church, ourselves, and others, imperiously demands that we should endeavor in the strength of our God to set up our banner here.

Obstacles to Overcome

That we have undertaken a work of no ordinary magnitude will appear from taking a view of the field itself.

The Situation of the Country

The region over which we are called to exercise a Presbyterian influence is in extent not less than one hundred and fifty miles square, containing a population of probably more than one hundred thousand souls, not generally collected into dense settlements, but scattered along the rivers, creeks, and rivulets which wind their way among the lofty mountains with which they are surrounded.

To accomplish the object we have in view, and to comply with our obligations to the Head of the church, we must not only calculate upon bringing the gospel to bear upon those who live in the thickly populated settlements, and where congregations are already organized, but upon those who are scattered over the whole region. Look at the huge and numerous mountains which lie in the way, many of which are almost impassable. Look also at the many bold and rapid streams which pass among them, and bear in mind that not a few of those to whom we are bound to preach the gospel live along the margin of these waters, which are often both difficult and dangerous to cross, and you can at once see that we have undertaken to accomplish a task of no ordinary character.

The Theological Prejudice of the Population

But the obstacles which the situation of the country presents are not the only, nor are they the main, difficulties with which we will have to contend. There are others greater than these. Not only will we have to contend with the pride of the natural heart, and the opposition to the gospel, which are characteristics of fallen man, but, in some places, with no small amount of prejudice against Presbyterianism. Not a few view it as a system of fatalism, alike derogatory to the character of God, and subversive of man's accountability; or they have been taught to consider it as only another name for infidelity. But, however strong these prejudices may be, I have never yet known them to have so firm a hold upon the mind that they will not, in a great measure, if not entirely, give way when the doctrines which are taught in the Confession of Faith, which we believe, and which we preach, are plainly presented to any people. They are very different from the caricatures of Presbyterianism which are too often exhibited by those who differ with us in doctrine.

The Depravity of the People

But if we had no such prejudices to encounter, still the doctrines of grace which we preach have always been offensive to the world. When they were taught by our Saviour and his apostles, they were violently opposed, and such has been the conduct of the world in all ages. The reason of this is plain: They stand directly opposed - to the pride of the natural heart, to the workings of the old man of sin in the soul. The world does not object to a system of religion which fosters the pride of the natural heart. It does not object to a system of religion which will bend to the spirit of this world, which will indulge in a full participation of all its amusements and pleasures. But a religion which points the sinner to his miserable and lost condition; which shows him that he is dead under the law — dead to all holy affection to God, and justly exposed to his everlasting displeasure; — a religion which has God for its author; which requires deep conviction of sin, evangelical sorrow for it, and an entire turning from it to God; which presses on the sinner holiness of heart and life, is one against which the corrupt heart will always revolt. As, then, we preach the doctrines of total depravity; the sinner's inability; regeneration by the free and unmerited grace of God; justification by the imputed righteousness of Christ; that faith is the gift of God; that the work of sanctification is carried on in the heart of the believer by the Spirit of God; that every true believer will persevere to the end; and that God has all the glory in the salvation of the sinner, we have to contend with no ordinary amount of opposition from the corruptions of the natural heart. But at this we are not to be surprised, when we know that these corruptions stand directly opposed to the whole gospel plan. Nor are we to be discouraged from preaching the truth; for, however strong and powerful this opposition may be, it can be made to fall by the sword of the Spirit. Whose opposition could be greater, or whose prejudices stronger, than were those of Paul? Yet how soon were they subdued by the grace of God!

Such are some of the difficulties with which we will have to contend in "setting up our banner" in this region of country.

The Means to Accomplish Our Sacred and Solemn Obligation

II. I come now to the second thing proposed, which is, to explain a little, the means we must use to accomplish this end.

Means are ordinarily a part of God's plan in the salvation of sinners; consequently no calculations can be made that they will be saved without them. But it is the spirit with which they are used, which, under God, gives them their efficacy. Unless they be used in the name and in the strength of our God — unless they be accompanied with an humble dependence upon him, and with submission to his holy will — they will not avail. The more completely we are stripped of every shadow of self-dependence in the use of the means, and trust alone to the arm of Heaven to aid us, the more certain we will be to succeed. This was David's hold. This was his strength when he engaged in an unequal contest with the Ammonites and Syrians. They trusted to idols to give them victory, but he trusted to the God of Israel, by whom he triumphed. But that eye which watched over David, and that arm which strengthened him, can alone crown our efforts with success. And just so far as he is with us, so far will we succeed in "setting up our banner" in opposition to all prejudices and false opinions which may exist in this region; and so far will we see sinners, through our humble instrumentality, brought to bow at the foot of the cross.

Laying this down as a fundamental point from which we must never deviate, I proceed to mention some of the means which we must use to effect the end we have in view:

Preach the Whole Truth Plainly

1. We must preach the gospel — by which I mean the whole truth; a plain exposition of the distinguishing doctrines of grace; the plain, practical principles of the Bible — in the plain, unsophisticated manner in which it is presented in this book.

It is well known that strong prejudices exist in the minds of not a few against some points in theology which, we believe, are contained in the Bible; such as the imputation of Adam's sin to his posterity; the sovereignty of God; his electing love in the salvation of the sinner; and the imputation of Christ's righteousness to the believer. Some, in order to avoid coming in contact with those prejudices, have, when expounding the gospel, measurably left these points out of view, although they admit that they are essentially connected with the divine plan. But how can this course be reconciled with truth and the conscience? How can it be reconciled with the matter of fact, that we are to declare the whole counsel of God?

But there are others who, whilst they do not fail to present these doctrines to the minds of their hearers, yet endeavor to explain them so as to make them more palatable; to make them conform more to the prejudices of the world, and, if possible, to allay their opposition, and have evidently explained them away altogether. We have no doubt that this is one way in which so much error has got into the church in this day.

It is entirely a mistaken idea to suppose that truth and religion can be promoted by accommodating them to the prejudices of the world; and that minister of Jesus Christ who endeavors to do this, does just so much to destroy the truth of the Bible, and the saving influences of religion on the hearts of impenitent sinners. The question with us is not, What will suit the prejudices of the world; but, What does the Bible say? What has God revealed? And whatever these are, we must preach them, whether the world will hear or whether they will forbear. Nor have we the least evidence to believe that our preaching will be successful in any other way. God is truth; his word is truth; and nothing but truth will ever succeed in the salvation of sinners.

Assume the Character of a Missionary

2. In the second place, in order that we may effect the grand object we have in view, each member of this presbytery must measurably

assume the character of a missionary. He must not calculate on spending his time exclusively in one or two congregations; but he must calculate upon making frequent 'excursions into destitute places. He must be willing to bear all the self-denial which will be necessary in leaving his own people, and encounter the fatigue which will be necessary that the gospel may be preached in every destitute part.

My brethren in the ministry, that we may engage with pleasure and usefulness in this arduous work, we must have our minds strongly impressed with the value of the souls whose salvation we seek. Indeed, nothing can give a more powerful stimulant to ministerial effort, than for the mind to act under the constant impression "that it will profit a man nothing if he should gain the whole world and lose his own soul" and yet, "that it pleaseth God through the foolishness of preaching to save them that believe." With these two ideas before the mind, shall we fear the labor? Or shall we fear success, when the great Head of the church has promised, "Lo, I am with you alway, even to the end of the world"?

I am aware that a difficulty may arise in the minds of some from this view of the subject. It may appear to be directly opposed to the solemn contract which exists between pastor and people, in which each party agrees to comply with the terms therein stipulated. If we estimate the value of preaching by dollars and cents, then would there be a violation of contract. But if we calculate from the good it may do, then is there no violation of contract, as the engagement from its very nature implies that the congregation should, for a short time, yield up the labors of their pastor, if it be probable that they will be more useful elsewhere. Add to this, if a minister be influenced by the proper spirit; if his heart be filled with the love of souls; if he feels an ardent desire to promote the interest of the Redeemer's kingdom, then may he do much of this labor through the week, and lose but few Sabbaths from his people.

Employ Additional Missionaries

3. In the third place, missionaries must be employed, who will make it their exclusive business to preach in those destitute places. The success which has attended this method of giving the gospel to the destitute gives it a preeminence over every other. It has been the means in the hand of God of doing much good. As a proof of this we have only to look at those flourishing churches in the West, many of which were organized by missionaries. Others, when weak and unable to support a pastor, were supplied by missionaries until they became able.

And there is no region in this vast valley, in which missionaries are more needed, and will be longer necessary, than within the bounds of this presbytery. The scattered state of the population in many places, and the impossibility from the situation of the country that it should ever be otherwise, render it improbable, not to say impossible, that they should ever be formed into such congregations as will be able to support a minister. And this is true, even upon the supposition that the people were generally inclined to Presbyterianism, which is by no means the case.

One main object, then, with this presbytery, must be to support missionaries. But the question arises, how is this to be done? A brief calculation will answer this question, and show that we can with ease sustain not less than two missionaries constantly in the field. Let each member of the churches pay annually twenty-five cents to this object. This, with the aid which we have a right to expect from the Board of Missions of the General Assembly, and the amount which can with ease be collected in the missionary field, will furnish a support to two or more missionaries, in constant service. Have we not a right to expect that our churches will heartily cooperate with us in the work? Will they not do more than, according to this calculation, they are called on to do?

Attend Presbytery Meetings

4. But the fourth and last thing that I shall mention on this point, is a punctual attendance of the members on the meetings of presbytery. Some may suppose that this can have but little influence in accomplishing the object we have in view; but, upon examination, it will be found to be a matter of vital importance. In all circumstances this is a most binding duty; and, as I understand our ordination vows, they place us under the most solemn obligations not to neglect it.

But if this be true in the general, it is still more important in our case. We are but few at best. Even the absence of one member will be felt. But the absence of a few will reduce us to a mere fraction. Then we will lose that weight of influence which we might otherwise have. The world will very much judge of our cause from the character which we as a presbytery sustain. And I shall despair of ever seeing the Presbyterian banner set up in this region should this duty be neglected.

Some seem to suppose that, as the business of the church can be done without them, it is only time and labor lost to attend her judicatories. Time in the general cannot be better spent. The interview which we have with one another; the sermons we hear preached; the interchange of sentiment and feelings in transacting the business of the church; and the united prayers which ascend to the throne of grace, all tend to enliven and animate the soul. And it not unfrequently occurs that the ministers and elders return home under a quickened influence, which is imparted to their respective congregations, and thus both pastor and people are benefited. This is not an imaginary representation, but a matter of practical understanding. If, then, we study our own interest, the interest of our people, and of the church at large; if we wish in the strength of our God to set up our banner, we must be punctual in attending the judicatories of the church.

Such, then, are some of the means we must use, in order that we may have the unspeakable pleasure of seeing the cause of God prospering through our instrumentality, and that we may be instrumental in setting up our banner.

A Brief View of the Rise and Progress of Presbyterianism in West Virginia

III. But this leads me to the third thing proposed, which is, by way of appendix, to give you a brief view of the rise and progress of Presbyterianism in this region, where we propose to set up our banner. Here it will be distinctly understood as being no part of my design to enter into a detail of the rise and progress of particular congregations, but simply to state a few things in general connected with this subject.

I have not been able to procure a single record or document which will throw even the least ray of light on the subject before me. It is not, then, to be presumed that I shall be able, with accuracy, to state the facts. All I can do is to state what I have collected from aged persons yet living, who, when young, were conversant with the first settlement of this country.

The Early Settlers and their Religion

So far as can be ascertained, the first white person visited these western waters in 1749, but no attempt was made to settle the country until 1760. The first settlement was mainly made on Muddy Creek, in this county, which was entirely cut off by the Indians in the year 1763. Whether the gospel was ever preached among these first settlers, or what were their religious opinions, I have not been able to ascertain. It was not before the year 1769 that a resettlement commenced. These second adventurers emigrated mainly from the Valley, in this State. They were all inclined to Presbyterianism, and some of them were members in the church. There is an old lady now living in the county of Monroe, nearly or quite one hundred years of age, who was among this number, and who was a professor of religion when she came into the country, and who, for more than eighty years, has manifested the life and power of religion in all her walk and conversation before the world. Being, not long since, asked if she regretted that she had embraced religion at so early a period in her life, her whole soul seemed to wake up, and she exclaimed: "Regret it! No. If I had a thousand years to spend upon this earth, I would wish to spend them all in the service of my God."

Early Missionaries

Soon after the settlement commenced, missionaries were sent into the country. The first so far as can be ascertained, was a Mr. Crawford, who, it is believed, came from the South Branch of the Potomac. The names of Frazer, Bead, and others, are mentioned, but of them we know nothing. There are persons now living who attribute their conversion to the instrumentality of those missionaries, and who, for more than sixty years, have proved faithful soldiers of the cross, and who have, indeed, been as burning and shining lights before the world.

As much danger was apprehended from the Indians at that time, the people were collected generally into forts, throughout this whole region of country. One of these stood on the spot where Lewisburg now stands, and but a few paces from this house; another, about eight miles from this place, called Donnelly's Fort. This fort was attacked by the Indians in May, 1778; and it is stated that, at the time when the news of this attack reached Lewisburg, there was a Presbyterian clergyman in the fort at this place, and, as he was shortly to leave the place, some of the parents were anxious to have their children baptized before he departed. About the time they were making preparations for administering the ordinance, the news of the assault reached them, and so great was the confusion which it produced, that some of the parents were about to present children who were not their own.

Early Churches and Pastors

In the year 1785 or '86, the Rev. John McCue settled near this place. He was the first minister of the gospel that ever resided in this region of country, except a Baptist brother who, I am told, was among the first settlers. It is believed that Mr. McCue organized the first churches ever formed of any denomination, not only on the western waters of Virginia, but in much the largest proportion of the Valley of the Mississippi. He organized three congregations — one in this neighborhood, one in the fork of Spring Creek, in this county, and one in what is now Monroe county. We regret that no record of this has been handed down to us. As far as can be ascertained, it was during his ministry in this county that the first Protestant church was built in any of those States which lie west of this. This house stood about one mile and a half or two miles from this place, on the land now owned by Mr. George Osborne, a spot sacred to the memory of Presbyterianism. Mr. McCue continued but a few years in this county. He removed to Augusta county, where he continued to preach until God called him from his labors.

He was succeeded by the Rev. Benjamin Grigsby, who came into this county in the year 1794. He preached to the united congregations of Lewisburg and Union. But no records are left to show what was done during his ministry in these congregations. He removed to Norfolk, where he ceased from his labors, when in the prime of life.

The Missionary Pastor

In March, 1808, I was sent by the Synod of Virginia as a missionary into this and the county of Monroe; and being invited to take charge of the united congregations of Lewisburg and Union, I removed to this place in June of the same year. There were at that time four elders in this congregation, and about fifteen or twenty members. In the Union congregation, one elder, and about the same number of members. In

Spring Creek, one elder, and, it is believed, six or eight members. This shows that in 1808 there were but three congregations on the western waters of Virginia, two of which had measurably ceased to exist, and in all numbered about fifty members. These congregations had been in a much more flourishing state; but as several years had elapsed from the time that Mr. Grigsby left them until I took charge of them, various circumstances concurred to cause their decline.

The Fruits of Their Labors

There are, at this time, in this presbytery, fifteen congregations; nine of these lie immediately on or near to Greenbrier River; one in Kanawha county; one at Point Pleasant; one in Parkersburg, in the county of Wood; another in a remote part of that county; one on French Creek, in Lewis county; and one in the county of Randolph; containing in all from twelve to fifteen hundred members.

Concluding Remarks

Such is the brief sketch which I have been able to collect on this important subject. But as I have not had recourse to any record or document whatever, this will be a sufficient apology for any mistake I may have made. But in connection with what I have said, I would make a few concluding remarks;

The Presbyterians Were Here First

1. It is clear, from the view I have given, that the Presbyterian banner was the first ever set up in this region of country. So far as is known to us, Presbyterians were the first who preached on these western waters, unless it were by the Baptist brother already alluded to. But be this as it may, there can be no doubt but that the first stand ever taken for the cause of God was made by the Presbyterians. They hoisted the first religious flag. They unfurled the first religious banner ever set up in this immense country. They struck the first stroke and

reared the first house ever consecrated to God in it. Here the first spark was kindled which has shed so much light over this western world. We, then, as a presbytery, have the honor of cultivating that field, in which the first spot was consecrated to God, — in a country vast in extent, — a country not surpassed for fertility, and prosperity by any other in the world, — a country where civil and religious despotism are not known, but where everyone is permitted to sit under his own vine and fig tree; and where the gospel has shed no small amount of its benign and heavenly influence. And shall we shrink at the obstacles which lie in our way? Shall we fear success? No; under the great Head of the church "we will set up our banners."

Be Encouraged by What Has Already Been Accomplished

2. Although Presbyterianism has progressed but slowly in the region in which we set up our banner; still, if we look at the situation of the country, the difficulties that were to be encountered, and the means employed to accomplish the end, the wonder will be that it succeeded at all. For some years preceding that of 1808, the people had but little Presbyterian preaching among them; and no small amount of effort had been made to prejudice them against it, and with no little success. I have been told by several persons, that when I first came into the county they considered it not only unnecessary, but wrong, to go to hear me preach, as they had been taught to believe that Presbyterianism was fatalism — or another name for infidelity. The current of prejudice was strong, and the opposition powerful. Now, for twelve or fifteen years there was but one Presbyterian preacher within the limits which this presbytery now occupies, who had to encounter all the fatigue which was necessary to preach the gospel from point to point; and to contend with all the prejudice and opposition which was made to the cause. The wonder then is, that it has progressed even as well as it has done. Evidently the hand of God has hitherto been with the church; and shall we now fear, when there

are ten to one engaged in preaching the word? and when there are thirty to one enlisted in the cause of their Divine Master? Shall we not rather take encouragement from what has been done, and go forth under the full assurance that God will be with us.

Difficult Circumstances Are Well-Calculated
to Foster Religion in the Heart

3. It is true that religion takes deep root in the heart very much in proportion to the dangers, conflicts and trials through which the believer may be called to pass. To be dandled on the lap of ease, and fondled in the arms of prosperity, often proves a snare to the soul. Hence we find, that those who have been subjected to the greatest trials often make the highest attainment in piety. Many of those who lived at that period in the church when persecution rose to its highest point, have exhibited religion in its true light before the world; have shown its power and efficacy to sustain the soul under the most excruciating bodily tortures, and to raise it above all the fears of death. How ardent was the piety, and how strong must have been the faith of those venerable martyrs who sealed the truth with their blood! Who can read their lives, and look at the death which they died, and not exclaim, "Let me die the death of the righteous, and let my last end be like his."

But the influence of religion is not confined to those dark ages of cruel persecution. Its effects are felt at all times, and under all the dangers and trials to which we may be subjected. Of this we have a full proof in the character and conduct of those who had to contend with the dangers and trials connected with the first settling of this country. Of these we can know but little. We may read the story, and hear the tale related, and feel something like terror and a glow of sympathy pass over the mind; but we cannot enter into the feelings of those who had them to encounter. We can very imperfectly understand the feelings of those who never for one moment, either by night or by day, considered themselves safe from the attacks of the cruel savage. But, however imperfectly we can enter into their feelings, we can understand that religion was the very thing to sustain the mind under such circumstances, and that the circumstances themselves were well calculated to foster religion in the heart, and to raise the mind to a high stand in piety. Such were their effects on some of the first settlers in this country. I have had the great pleasure to have had no little intercourse with some of those whose souls were tried with these dangers, and I can confidently say that I have never met with any whose piety was more ardent, whose love to their Saviour was stronger, and who manifested more of the life and spirit of religion in all their walk and conversation before the world. How many are the sweet counsels I have had with them, and how often have they administered consolation to my mind when sinking under the trials which I had to meet in my work!

Let Making Converts to the Faith Be Our Highest Ambition

Let it, then, my brethren, be our highest ambition, under the great Head of the church, to make converts to the faith, whose lives will correspond with the first germs of Presbyterianism which sprung up in this region. Let us not only endeavor "in the name of our God to set up our banners," but to enlist such soldiers as will honor it; such as will exhibit its beauty, glory, and excellency before the world; who, from every step they take, and every effort they make, will show that they have been with Christ. And may the great Head of the church make us useful to this end!

APPENDIX B

Suggestions for the New River Presbytery
of the Presbyterian Church in America

After reading carefully all that has come before, I hope that the Presbytery will prayerfully consider the following suggestions:

1. That the Presbytery emphasize the importance of identifying or raising up ministerial candidates from within the boundaries of the New River Presbytery.

2. That the Candidates and Credentials Committee develop a careful method for overseeing the care of candidates and advancing their progress toward licensure and ordination.

3. That the Presbytery develop a program to teach and train ministers after the Log College or mentor/tutor model of the early Presbyterians, under the oversight of the Candidates and Credentials Committee.[1]

4. That the Candidates and Credentials Committee develop a curriculum for the program that accords with the Uniform Curriculum Guide of the Presbyterian Church in America.[2]

5. That the Presbytery call and support a Teaching Elder to

---

[1] For example, see my "An Unobstructed Educational Model for Ministerial Candidates of the New River Presbytery of the Presbyterian Church in America" (Doctor of Ministry thesis, Pittsburgh Theological Seminary, 2016). Additionally, Dr. Brian Kelso made a strong case for the legitimacy of non-traditional training programs for presbyterian ordination in "Credentialing for the Gospel Ministry" (white paper, Lamp Theological Seminary, n.d), accessed December 6, 2018, www.lampseminary.org.

[2] The PCA should consider revising the Uniform Curriculum Guide to bring it more in line with modern pedagogical theory. As it stands, it is limited in its usefulness for the construction of presbytery-level educational programs.

administrate this program, mentor/tutor students, and raise and administrate funds to support himself and the program, and to subsidize students, under the oversight of the Candidates and Credentials Committee.

6. That the Presbytery develop a Ministerial Internship with emphasis upon the unique sociological aspects of Appalachia in general and West Virginia in particular, under the oversight of the Credentials Committee.

7. That the Presbytery revive the "Licentiate as Probationer" model utilized by the early Presbyterians of West Virginia, with the goals 1) that they itinerate regularly throughout the state's current churches, 2) that they strategically itinerate in unreached territories with an eye for starting new churches and developing calls, and 3) that they fulfill the conditions of an ordainable internship, geared toward the unique ministry-context of West Virginia.

8. That the Presbytery request and encourage its churches to prayerfully and financially support the program and its students and to identify potential candidates to participate in the program.

9. That the administrator pursue official links to seminaries (e.g., Reformed Theological Seminary) to offer field-based, for-credit, adjunct instruction in Appalachian Studies, as well as Ministerial Internships with Appalachian focus to students of these seminaries.

ABOUT THE AUTHOR

Dennis Eldon Bills is a proud, eighth-generation West Virginian. He is a minister in the New River Presbytery of the Presbyterian Church in America and works bivocationally as a family law mediator and college educator. He received a BA and MA from Bob Jones University, an MEd from Covenant College, and a DMin from Pittsburgh Theological Seminary. He and his wife Kathi have three grown children.

Dennis is the author or editor of *How to Preach with an Interpreter: A Crash Course* (Wipf and Stock, 2010), *A Church You Can See: Building a Case for Church Membership* (ReformingWV Publications, 2017), and *The Captives of Abb's Valley: Revised and Annotated* (ReformingWV Publications, 2019).

Made in United States
North Haven, CT
04 November 2022

26302652R00124